The
Reference Shelf®

Whistleblowers

The Reference Shelf
Volume 87 • Number 2
H.W. Wilson
Published by
GREY HOUSE PUBLISHING
Amenia, New York
2015

The Reference Shelf

The books in this series contain reprints of articles, excerpts from books, addresses on current issues, and studies of social trends in the United States and other countries. There are six separately bound numbers in each volume, all of which are usually published in the same calendar year. Numbers one through five are each devoted to a single subject, providing background information and discussion from various points of view and concluding with an index and comprehensive bibliography that lists books, pamphlets, and articles on the subject. The final number of each volume is a collection of recent speeches. Books in the series may be purchased individually or on subscription.

Publisher's Cataloging-In-Publication Data
(Prepared by The Donohue Group, Inc.)

Whistleblowers / [compiled by H. W. Wilson]. -- [First edition].

   pages : illustrations ; cm. -- (The reference shelf ; volume 87, number 2)

   Edition statement supplied by publisher.
   Includes bibliographical references and index.
   ISBN: 978-1-61925-691-0 (v. 87, no. 2)
   ISBN: 978-1-61925-689-7 (volume set)

   1. Whistleblowing--Sources.   2. Whistleblowing--Law and legislation--Sources.   3. Disclosure of information--Sources.   4. Corruption--Prevention--Sources. 5. Crime--Prevention--Sources. I. H.W. Wilson Company. II. Series: Reference shelf ; v. 87, no. 2.

JF1525.W45 W457 2015
364.4/1

Cover: Barton Gellman/ Getty Images News/ Getty Images
Introductions: Richard Klin

Printed in Canada

Contents

2

Confronting Perpetrators

3

Reprisals and the Law

4

Security in Democracy

Preface

In the 1970s, the nation was riveted by emerging evidence that the administration of Richard Nixon had engaged in a series of corrupt activities on a massive, national scale. Much of these revelations were transmitted via the reporting of the *Washington Post*'s Bob Woodward and Carl Bernstein.

Woodward and Bernstein had an anonymous source, a prominent figure in government who spilled some of the administration's deepest, darkest secrets. The reporters, uncompromising about preserving this man's anonymity, famously dubbed him Deep Throat. It was Deep Throat who led Woodward and Bernstein on the investigative path that culminated in Richard Nixon's resignation in 1974. (Decades later it was revealed that Deep Throat was Mark Felt, a higher-up in the FBI.)

Deep Throat, in essence, was a whistleblower. The very term *whistleblower* has a huge range. Whistleblowing can have grand, national—and international—consequences as in the Nixon scandal and, in more recent times, in the high-profile cases of Edward Snowden, Julian Assange, and Chelsea Manning (known as Bradley Manning until her gender and name change announcement in 2013). Whistleblowers have uncovered systemic fraud at Wall Street financial institutions and myriad violations in the world of college sports. Karen Silkwood, who in the 1970s revealed shocking safety gaps in a nuclear-power plant—and paid for these revelations with her life—was the subject of a movie starring Meryl Streep. Erin Brockovich—the subject of a movie starring Julia Roberts—alerted the public to serious cases of harmful environmental contamination. Indeed, the list of whistleblower-movies is a lengthy one that includes *Serpico* (1973), *The Insider* (1999), *The Constant Gardener* (2005), *Michael Clayton* (2007), *The Whistleblower* (2010), and *Citizenfour*, the 2014 Academy Award–winning documentary on Edward Snowden. Whistleblowing, though, doesn't have to be so high-profile as to warrant books or movies. Whistleblowers can be found in the office, on the school board, in the family business, all with potentially high stakes. Whistleblowers often risk their livelihoods, their social standing, their families' futures—and sometimes their physical safety.

What is whistleblowing? As with any multifaceted issue, the definition varies depending on point of view. Although to some the term has come to have unpleasant connotations, akin to being a snitch, in the early 1970s, the pioneering consumer advocate Ralph Nader used the term to mean something not just respectable, but vital: a point of pride. The web site of Whistleblowing-CEE provides a commonly used explanation: when a current or former member of an organization discloses "illegal, immoral, or illegitimate practices under the control of their employers to persons or organizations that may be able to effect action."

"This is the age of the whistleblower," Matt Taibbi wrote in *Rolling Stone* (February 18, 2015). "[W]histleblowers are becoming to this decade what rock stars were to the Sixties—pop culture icons, global countercultural heroes." *Time* magazine designated whistleblowers as persons of the year for 2002, including Coleen Rowley, who accused the FBI of failing to detect the signs of the impending attack on the World Trade Center in 2001; Cynthia Cooper, "a WorldCom internal auditor, [who] alerted the company's board. . . to $3.8 billion in accounting irregularities. A month later, the telecommunications giant declared the largest bankruptcy in U.S. history;" and Sherron Watkins, who "sent memos in August 2001 warning Enron chairman Kenneth Lay that improper accounting could cause the company to collapse." The company later filed for bankruptcy and suffered lasting notoriety. (Jamie Holguin, *CBS News*, December 22, 2002)

The resurgence of whistleblowing stems, in large part, from innovations and social changes that undergirded the 1960s and 1970s, which left a populace less inclined to accept the word of those in power. There was also the strong sense that something was amiss in the halls of government and in corporate boardrooms: the president was engaged in criminal activities; the FBI was spying on its own citizens; the environment was being destroyed. The prevalent corruption in political and social institutions has provided plenty of fodder for would-be whistleblowers.

Rolling Stone makes another, crucial point: ". . . one of America's ugliest secrets is that our own whistleblowers often don't do so well after the headlines fade and cameras recede. The ones who don't end up in jail. . . or in exile. . . often still go through years of harassment and financial hardship." In the financial sector, many whistleblowers "have seen their evidence disappeared into cushy settlement deals that let corporate wrongdoers off the hook with negligible fines."

Whistleblowing-CEE makes the key distinction that whistleblowers are not informants. "Informants are often involved in some sort of unethical affair, and use disclosure for clarifying their own role, or reduce their liability. Governments often offer the chance of pardoning the crimes of people who report malpractices which they were involved in." In other words, whistleblowers take on a great risk.

The motivations, circumstances, and consequences of whistleblowing are varied and far-ranging. "The question of when to remain quiet and when to speak out—and how to do it," Alisa Tugend reported in the September 20, 2013, *New York Times*, "can be extraordinarily difficult no matter what the situation." Luckily, according to Tugend, some significant steps have been taken to cushion whistleblowers from any potential damage to their lives and career. There has been "legislation rewarding whistleblowers for coming forth and protecting them against retaliation. The most prominent of those is the Dodd-Frank Act, which passed in 2010." However, "in 2009, 4 percent of those who said they experienced reprisals for reporting wrongdoing cited physical threats to themselves or their property. In 2011, that rose to 31 percent." Thirty-one percent is a staggering statistic.

Retaliation against whistleblowing takes many shapes. Tom Devine and Tarek F. Maassarani have chronicled responses from the corporate sector, beginning with the enforced assumption that "the power of the organization is stronger than the power of the individual—even individuals who have truth on their side." There is the smokescreen tactic: "attacking the source's motives, credibility, professional competence, or virtually anything else that will work to cloud an issue." Another tactic is the formal reprimand, or isolating whistleblowers "by forcing them to work from home or take administrative leave with or without pay." Whistleblowers can be reorganized out of a job, or blacklisted so that they will never find comparable employment. The list goes on, and although great strides have been made, whistleblowing is still a risky business.

Some raise the point that whistleblowers might have a personal agenda, and be motivated by gripes against a nasty boss or coworker. Tugend quotes Stuart Sidle, the director of the Industrial-Organizational Psychology program at the University of New Haven in Connecticut: "I question someone trying to report externally before reporting internally. . . It's too easy, now, to put up a video of bad behavior on YouTube or lash out on Facebook without ever speaking with the people who might be willing to resolve the problems." Indeed, the Security Exchange Commission's whistleblower program encourages employees to report malfeasance through internal channels first. In the end, most would agree that if the offenses are grave enough, personal motivations are irrelevant.

This volume contains a broad array of whistleblowing. Key topics include privacy rights, legal freedom, the nature of dissent, and matters concerning the media. Whether reading about the high-profile cases of Snowden and Manning or cases that will never reach the Supreme Court, the reader will discover a broad spectrum of opinion on these issues, issues that are certain to continue to dominate the national discourse.

Bibliography

Devine, Tom, and Tarek F. Maassarani. *The Corporate Whistleblower's Survival Guide* (San Francisco: Barrett-Koehler, 2011).

Holguin, Jamie. "Whistleblowers Honored by Time." *CBS News*, December 22, 2002; http://www.cbsnews.com/news/whistleblowers-honored-by-time/

Taibbi, Matt. "A Whistleblower's Horror Story. *Rolling Stone*, February 18, 2015; http://www.rollingstone.com/politics/news/a-whistleblowers-horror-story-20150218?page=2

Tugend, Alina. "Opting to Blow the Whistle or Choosing to Walk Away." *New York Times*, September 20, 2013.

Whistleblowing-CEE Web site. "What Is Whistleblowing?" http://www.whistleblowing-cee.org/about_whistleblowing/

1
Ethical Obligations

© Bill Clark/CQ-Roll Call Group/Getty Images

Community activist and whistleblower Frederick Newell testifies during the House Oversight and Government Reform Committee's Economic Growth, Job Creation, and Regulatory Affairs Subcommittee and House Judiciary Committee's Constitution and Civil Justice Subcommittee joint hearing on "The DOJ's Quid Pro Quo with St. Paul: A Whistleblower's Perspective," on Tuesday, May 7, 2013.

Building an Ethical Framework

The difficulties in deciding to go public and become a whistleblower are many. There is the concern of appearing credible, the understandable fear of retaliation, the worry over how one's livelihood or family will be affected. And then there are the vast internal struggles. "The whistleblower," Kirsty Matthewson writes, "is ultimately torn between loyalty to their employer (or the subject of their revelation) and their moral commitment to the law and society at large." Yet there is a consideration that is perhaps the most complicated of all: Is one *obligated* to report wrongdoing or criminal activity? Is silence a form of complicity? What framework is the potential whistleblower required—or not—to follow?

Some colleges and universities have mandatory honor codes—in which a student is required to report any cheating he or she may observe. Failure to do so results in a penalty sometimes as grave as the cheating itself. Lawyers and doctors are obligated to bring to light any cases of professional misconduct or outright malpractice. Although this often doesn't ease the burden on the whistleblower, there are procedures and precedent to fall back on, and if not procedure, a strong, entrenched sense of moral and professional obligation. "Many individual professionals," Myron Peretz Glazer and Penina Migdal Glazer have written, "have internalized the best of the professional ideology and remain deeply dedicated to serving the public good. Certain practitioners have always done outstanding pro bono work, served the poor, and insisted on the highest quality of service." *Do no harm*, after all, is the basic building block of medical ethics. The first canon of the code of National Society of Professional Engineering is that "the health, safety, and welfare of the public are to be placed first." (Mathieu Bouville, "Whistle-blowing and Morality") And then Myron and Penina Glazer add a caveat: "But advancement in the profession has not usually depended on such strict adherence to ideal standards." And, unfortunately, most cases when the whistleblower needs to step forward are rarely black and white and rarely as simple as adhering to professional guidelines.

The question of where an individual obtains that courage to risk potentially all will ultimately remain just that: a question. Myron and Penina Glazer discovered, not surprisingly, that individuals "who have a highly developed alternative belief system can withstand the intense pressure to conform. . . " The belief system can be a religious orientation or a strict, unshakable moral code.

More often than not, it is an innate sense that something is fundamentally wrong. "A whistle blower once testified in a California court about how his boss had regularly ordered him to discard some of the company's toxic waste into a local storm drain rather than dispose of it properly," relate Judy Nadler and Miriam Schulman (Markkula Center for Applied Ethics). "Why, the judge wanted to know, had the man finally decided to step forward after having participated in this illegal dumping for years. 'Well,' the man explained, 'I was fishing with my grandson, and it suddenly occurred to me that the waste I was dumping was going to pollute the water so that he might never be able to go fishing with his grandson.'"

Whistleblowers also correct behavior or procedures that shouldn't be in existence in the first place. "The certification of company accounts by senior executives should be a non-event," the August 15, 2002, *Economist* opined. Financial statements have long been considered the authoritative. straightforward source to ascertain the health—good or bad—of a company. But corporate America, these last few decades, has been hit with one damaging scandal after another. (The film *Wall Street*, after all, is not about financial acumen, but about crime.) "America," *The Economist* concluded, "no longer trusts its. . . leaders to tell the truth without being warned by the sound of prison doors slamming."

Daniel Ellsberg was a brilliant defense analyst in the 1960s who attained a high level of responsibility in matters relating to American involvement in Vietnam. As the war went on, he became convinced of its catastrophic effect and went to enormous trouble and even greater risk to leak reams of confidential information to the *New York Times*. These were the Pentagon Papers—one of the single most famous instances of whistleblowing in American history. Ellsberg made the case that "there is no substitute for hard evidence: documents, photographs, transcripts." (And today, of course, there is the Web, which has assumed increasing prominence when it comes to transmitting the work of whistleblowers.) "Often the only way for the public to get such evidence is if a dedicated public servant decides to release [the information] without permission. . . Leakers are often accused of being partisan, and undoubtedly many of them are. But the measure of their patriotism should be the accuracy and the importance of the information they reveal."

There are, however, some guidelines and assistance. The whistleblower, contrary to some opinion, actually does have the law on his or her side. Contracts or confidentiality agreements—in the context of nefarious activities—need not be honored. It's a crucial point: If the whistleblower is revealing illegal activity, he or she is providing a service. "Confidentiality contracts are not legitimate and should not be regarded to be ethically or legally operative," writes Ben O'Neill of the Mises Institute, "when the confidentiality is *designed to protect secret unlawful actions* that are being taken by one of the parties." O'Neill continues: "Broadly speaking, contracts cannot be regarded as legitimate if they involve agreement to perform an unlawful action, or an action designed to further an unlawful purpose. This is the basis on which one can regard whistleblowing as a lawful activity. . . . "

As per Jayne O'Donnell in *USA Today* (July 29, 2004), "Whistleblowers persist because that's the way they are—a breed apart, driven by a desire to expose dirty executives, protect consumers or avenge wrongs they feel have been done to them." Quite simply, it is a moral imperative: a sense of right and wrong. In many respects, whistleblowing is a logical continuation of childhood ethics: Play fair. Don't lie. Don't cheat. And certainly don't steal.

"Professional ethics is in fact professional morality," writes Mathieu Bouville. "Yet the dreadful retaliations against the messengers of the truth make it necessary to bring the needs of the whistle blower back into the picture." The brutal realities of going public can cancel out any moral formulations.

How do whistleblowers come to their decision to go public? Adam Waytz, James Dungan, and Liane Young conducted a study in which a "group of 74 research participants" were instructed "to write a paragraph about an occasion when they witnessed unethical behavior and reported it (and why), and. . . another group, of 61 participants," was asked "to write about an occasion when they witnessed unethical behavior and kept their mouths shut. . . the whistle-blowers used 10 times as many terms related to *fairness* and *justice*, whereas non-whistle-blowers used twice as many terms related to *loyalty*." The study highlighted the conflict between the desire to do good—to right the wrong—and the loyalty to the team. Often the whistleblower is exposing coworkers or supervisors, potentially putting the entire institution in a bad light. And other studies, interestingly, indicated that the focus of liberals is fairness, and loyalty is a more important criterion to conservatives.

One way to reduce the complexities of whistleblowing is, quite obviously, to eliminate the factors that make whistleblowing necessary in the first place. Lilanthi Ravishankar, also writing for the Markkula Center for Applied Ethics, lays out a convincing organizational blueprint—preventing whistleblowing by *encouraging* whistleblowing. If there is something seemingly counter-intuitive about this concept, there is also the practical application, which stems from a visceral question: How many of us would wish to be a part of a company or organization where whistleblowing is necessary? Ravishankar lays out some concrete steps: including "formal mechanisms for reporting violations," an explicit policy against any sort of retaliation, "clear communications about the process of voicing concerns, such as a specific chain of command," and a top-down endorsement that encourages a climate of support for any potential whistleblowing. Issues of right or wrong aside, there are also bottom-line considerations to buttress this open, encouraging attitude. "[C]ompanies are increasingly realizing that transparency and good business practices," Matthias Kleinhempel writes, "both provide sound competitive advantages and minimize public exposure risks. . . ."

Whistleblowing cannot be untethered from a reformer's ethos. "Few understand," Brian Penny writes in *Fast Company,* "that they . . . are whistleblowers every time they suggest a change or improvement at work." It is an enlightened, proactive framework: "Snitching on other employees may be seen as sinister, and your people may be embarrassed to speak up. Ensure you have a form, inbox, or number they can contact for anonymous tips. The police have prevented and solved a lot of crimes with this way; your business could flourish from anonymous tips as well." Furthermore, according to *The Economist* (January 10, 2002), "the American government claims that most of the billions of dollars that it retrieves from those who defraud federal agencies come via whistleblowers' reports. Many investigations carried out by antitrust authorities into illegal cartels, such as the recent vitamin price-fixing case in Europe, are initiated by reports from whistleblowers." It's an enlightened attitude, and whether adopting this attitude will become the norm among the powerful is an open question.

The many questions of whether to be a whistleblower—or not—unfortunately can't be resolved by the outside world. Certainly there are strictures: One needs to determine, first, that the motives for going public are not fueled by personal grudges, a desire to get even, or a thirst for fame (or infamy). And the potential whistleblower has to be absolutely certain he or she has explored every avenue of internal redress.

The ethical considerations of what—or not—to do carry the special burden that always exists: The burden of the internal struggle. And—ultimately—the sober conclusion is that the internal struggle is resolved alone.

Bibliography

Bouville, Mathieu. "Whistle-blowing and Morality." *Journal of Business Ethics;* http://mathieu.bouville.name/education-ethics/Bouville-whistle-blowing.pdf

Ellsberg, Daniel. "Truths Worth Telling." *New York Times,* September 28, 2004; http://www.nytimes.com/2004/09/28/opinion/28ellsberg.html?_r=0

Glazer, Myron Peretz, and Penina Migdal Glazer. *The Whistleblowers: Exposing Corruption in Government and Industry* (New York: Basic Books, 1989).

"In Praise of Whistleblowers." *The Economist,* January 10, 2002; http://www.economist.com/node/930052

"In Search of Honesty." *The Economist,* August 15, 2002; http://www.economist.com/node/1284261

Kleinhempel, Matthias. "Whistleblowers May Have Moral and Immoral Motivations." In Berlatsky, Noah, ed. *Whistleblowers* (Farmington Hills, MI: Greenhaven Press, 2012).

Matthewson, Kirsty. "Ethics and Whistleblowing." Expolink Web site, January 10, 2012; http://expolink.co.uk/whistleblowing/blog/ethics-and-whistleblowing/

Nadler, Judy, and Miriam Schulman. "Whistleblowing in the Public Sector." Markkula Center for Applied Ethics, Santa Clara University Web site; http://www.scu.edu/ethics/practicing/focusareas/government_ethics/introduction/whistleblowing.html

O'Donnell, Jayne. "Whistle-blowers Form a Breed Apart." *USA Today,* July 29, 2004; http://usatoday30.usatoday.com/money/companies/management/2004-07-29-whistle-blower-main_x.htm

O'Neill, Ben. "The Ethics of Whistleblowing." Mises Institute Web site, July 8, 2013; http://mises.org/library/ethics-whistleblowing

Penny, Brian. "Why You Should Encourage Whistleblowing at Your Company." *Fast Company,* May 30, 2014; http://www.fastcompany.com/3031223/5-ways-to-actually-make-whistleblowing-work-for-your-business

Ravishankar, Lilanthi. "Encouraging Internal Whistleblowing in Organizations." Markkula Center for Applied Ethics, Santa Clara University Web site; http://www.scu.edu/ethics/publications/submitted/whistleblowing.html

Waytz, Adam, James Dungan, and Liane Young. "The Whistle-Blower's Quandary." *New York Times,* August 2, 2013; http://www.nytimes.com/2013/08/04/opinion/sunday/the-whistle-blowers-quandary.html

I Had to Do It

By David Morgan
New Internationalist, April 1, 2014

Think of films like *All the President's Men*, *Erin Brockovich* and *The Insider*.

These all tell the stories of whistleblowers whose place in the hall of fame seems assured. Through their disclosures they, rather than governments and leaders, have become the important ones.

But for most of the people I have seen—since becoming a volunteer consultant for a whistleblower charity—it is a very different story.

Most experience loss, not gain, through their actions. They have had their lives turned upside down, their places in their communities dismantled. They have lost their peace of mind and quite often faith in their own value and motives, as well as those of others.

So what motivates a whistleblower? Why risk so much?

Traitor or Hero?

As a term, "whistleblower" sounds vaguely pejorative—like a snitch. I prefer "social discloser". In Germany there is no word for it; the expression used there translates as "traitor".

In totalitarian states, like North Korea or Iran, hideous consequences for any perceived betrayals are to be expected. In the mature democracies of Europe, North America or Australasia, we expect a different set of mores.

But I am struck by the harshness of our societal attitudes towards those who break public laws or standards and undermine assumptions about the safety of our world.

Take the vehicle maker who discovers that his factory has been using seriously substandard materials. The economic impact of a scandal on his company, already on the brink of collapse, would be disastrous. He is in a position to make himself and all his colleagues unemployed. But he is also aware that the lives of vehicle users are at risk. He talks to, and is shunned by, his union and his bosses. But still he speaks out.

He receives death threats by mail and loses his job. His health begins to deteriorate. He is accused of having mental-health problems, which, of course, by now, he does. He goes to his member of parliament and is told that there is "no evidence" to support his claims. The MP and local newspapers are funded by interested parties.

Think of the health workers who have spoken out about the effects of spending cuts and the culture of un-care that prevails in some British hospitals and nursing homes.

People like Margy Haywood, a nurse who, for the BBC's Panorama programme, covertly filmed the abuse and neglect of elderly patients in an NHS hospital. It was she who was punished, losing her nursing registration for "breaching confidentiality" while the staff who were abusing the patients were allowed to carry on working.

The emotional fall-out from revealing truths that others prefer to keep hidden is frequently underestimated. There will be powerful forces ranged against the discloser in order to maintain the status quo. Disclosers threaten the defenses and belief systems that institutions have developed to permit the behavior that is being exposed. Revelations can be experienced by the institution and colleagues within it as humiliating and attacking. These colleagues may see themselves as justified in retaliating against a whistleblower and there may be a concerted effort to discredit or pathologize her or him.

Paranoia?

"Is this place bugged?" asked the first discloser I worked with, referring to my consulting room.

Normally I would see such a concern as a fantasy, a projected form of aggression, externalized on to the outside world, where it then persecutes the originator from outside, in the minds of others or through delusions and hallucinations. Through externalization, the internal aggressive impulses are thus reduced and "put out to tender".

But when it comes to social disclosers the question "is my room bugged?" does not seem so delusional.

Undoubtedly, some of the people I see do exist in paranoid states of mind and some will have had traces of this before they disclosed. After they have blown the whistle they feel watched, their level of trust is low and it is easy to write them off as vexatious litigants and troublemakers.

Of course, not all whistleblowing is benign or altruistically motivated. Disclosure can be used to inflict revenge and humiliation. Stalled careers, failed love affairs or lack of a pay rise can increase the willingness of some individuals to shame or punish their communities, employers or families. But these are a small minority, in my view.

What is more likely is that the organization called into question by the whistleblower becomes dedicated to destroying the moral individual—and often succeeds. Disclosers are broken, unable to reconcile their actions and beliefs with the responses they receive from others.[1]

In order to make sense of their stories, some whistleblowers must set aside the things they have always believed. For example: that truth is larger than the herd instinct; that someone in charge will do the right thing; that the family is a haven from a heartless world.

Any psychoanalyst will tell you that we project on to external authorities our internal versions of parental figures. When those parental figures are benign and fair-minded the failure of external authorities to live up to the projection can be devastating. Many whistleblowers recover from their experience but even then they live in a world very different from the one they knew before their confrontation with the organization.

Many people who disclose reasonably might expect some reward, praise, respect.

They often face disappointment. Often, we just don't want to know. Some receive support from their loved ones, others can feel persecuted by them, as they feel guilty or are made to feel that way for putting their families at risk.

It is useful for the whistleblower to have an understanding of group hostility to revelations that are threatening to cohesion. The discloser needs to find a way to maintain their [his or her] self-belief during these times of personal stress and marginalization.

They will also need help to understand the unconscious reasons for putting themselves in this situation in the first place.

Unable to Double

And that takes us to the heart of individual psychology, personal experience and unconscious motivation. Any previous emotional and psychological difficulties will be exacerbated or brought to the surface. Motives and personal integrity will be publicly questioned. Through reversal and projection the institution that is being called into question can evade any sense of responsibility for wrong-doing. The discloser is therefore made to feel that she or he is the wrongdoer, arousing serious self-doubt and depression.

In his book *1984* George Orwell used the term "double-think". The psychological phenomenon behind this is called 'doubling'. For example, you are a middle-level functionary in a bureaucracy or corporation and you possess some truth that you know does not conform to the agenda of your institution or boss.

Doubling—or "splitting" as I would call it as a psychoanalyst—means you can hold true to your personal morality while maintaining a separate public or institutional morality. At home you may never behave this way but at work telling the truth may hurt not only your institution but your livelihood and the health and safety of your family. In such situations, it is helpful to be able to hold contradictory positions to separate out your different selves and different loyalty structures. As US psychologist Fred Alford has noted, whistleblowers are often people who are unable to "split" themselves. The inherent contradiction would be too great and too painful.

German philosopher Hannah Arendt wrote of heroic individuals, people who talk seriously with themselves about what they are doing, people who cannot double, or do double-speak. They feel a compulsion to do the "right thing".

As one patient told me: "I had to do it, I couldn't live with myself if I didn't speak up."

The Bigger Picture

"A market economy thrives on inequality so self-interest will always triumph over the moral good," observes philosopher, psychoanalyst and cultural critic Slavoj Zizek.

The whistleblower has to be vilified lest she or he expose the rottenness that we accept to maintain lifestyles often based on the suffering of others. Their lone voice is fulfilling a role in society that we are afraid to take.

We are never going to be able fully to decipher the motives of those who disclose. I am not sure we need to. We can argue about the personal stories of famous examples like Edward Snowden and Julian Assange.

Perhaps the most important thing to keep in mind is that societies which cannot tolerate disclosure and transparency are on their way to being totalitarian states. Whistleblowers therefore act as the conscience for us all.

What Motivates a Whistleblower?

By Meredith Melnick
The Huffington Post, October 7, 2014

A couple of recent news events brought whistleblowers into the spotlight. Last week, an anonymous whistleblower's report that President Obama took an elevator ride with a man who had a violent criminal record and was armed at the time, unbeknownst to the Secret Service, contributed to the resignation of the agency's director. Preceding that, ProPublica published an intricate story detailing the New York State Fed's cozy relationship to Goldman Sachs using accounts from a former employee who recently filed a wrongful termination lawsuit—what she and her legal team allege was a retaliatory step after she attempted to report misconduct.

Seemingly, instances of bad behavior by our government institutions become public knowledge only when an outraged employee publicizes them. But what distinguishes these employees from the many others with equal proximity to, but no urge to report, the malfeasance they see?

According to Janet P. Near, a professor at the Kelley School of Business at Indiana University who has studied whistleblowing since 1980, it's less about the psychology of the individual and more about the severity of the situation they've uncovered. "People look for differences in personality, background, but there aren't very large differences," Near told The Huffington Post. "What seems to predict whether someone will actually blow the whistle is: how serious the wrongdoing is, if they are very sure it happened and so on . . . Situational characteristics rather than personal ones."

Fully 45 percent of employees in the business sector see some type of misconduct and 64 percent of those do report it, according to a 2013 report from the Ethics Resource Center. That's quite a few people—nearly none of whom go on to media infamy like Edward Snowden and Chelsea Manning did.

Highly visible cases become that way, Near explained, most typically because a whistleblower has faced retaliation internally and must seek help outside the organization. And anyway, she wouldn't characterize Snowden as a whistleblower since he was not an employee of the agency he reported for misconduct.

"If they cannot suffer retaliation from their employer, we don't count them," said Near. "When the federal government retaliates against Snowden, they are not retaliating against a former employee—they are retaliating against a U.S. citizen. He was acting more as a journalist or other outsider with information about an organization."

Employment is an important defining characteristic of whistleblowing simply because employee retaliation is formidable—particularly in the small, specialized industries, where everyone knows each other. Sherron Watkins, the Enron vice president who was called before Congress to testify against her employer, faced difficulty finding employment thereafter, according to Near. Carmen Segarra, a former employee of the New York Federal Reserve, was fired after seven months on the job.

"Most of us grow up to realize that what people say and what people do are two things. We learn a certain cynicism about life, like that everything a politician promises isn't necessarily going to be what he does," C. Frederick Alford, political psychology professor and author of *Whistleblowers: Broken Lives and Organizational Power* told *Mother Jones*. "I think whistleblowers somehow come late to this realization. They're naive in a certain sense, and then when they come to realize that people are lying, cheating, stealing, whatever, they're shocked."

What Really Drives a Whistleblower Like Edward Snowden?

By Maggie Severns
Mother Jones, June 13, 2013

After Edward Snowden went public as the man who leaked the NSA's secret surveillance system to the country via a 12-minute video interview with the *Guardian,* questions immediately sprang up around his motivation for whistleblowing, his personal life, and whether his background is what he claims it to be.

Why is suspicion and distrust the natural reaction? Because a lot rests on whether Snowden is telling the truth, yes, but also because most of us (perhaps nearly everyone but whistleblowers themselves) have trouble understanding exactly what motivates a whistleblower. As University of Maryland political psychology professor C. Frederick Alford notes, humans are tribal beings, and even though society considers whistleblowers brave in theory, in practice there tends to be a sense of discomfort with those who break from the tribe.

Alford has spent more than a decade asking why some people reveal government secrets in the name of public good while most don't, asking what makes Edward Snowden Edward Snowden, and not one of the many other Booz Allen analysts who presumably saw the same information that Snowden did but kept quiet about it. Alford's 2001 book, *Whistleblowers: Broken Lives and Organizational Power,* examines the psychology of whistleblowing based on the extensive time he spent with people who've done it—some to much fanfare, others to very little. He says he's received a phone call or an email from a whistleblower about every month since the book came out 12 years ago, and in many cases has kept up for years with those who reach out. He spoke with *Mother Jones* about the Edward Snowden–Daniel Ellsberg parallel, why whistleblowers tend to have big egos, and what Snowden might face in the coming weeks and months.

Mother Jones: Based on what we know about Edward Snowden so far, does he remind you of other whistleblowers you've spent time with or studied over the years?

C. Frederick Alford: Daniel Ellsberg, overwhelmingly. I don't think Bradley Manning: Bradley Manning committed a data dump. He just released tons of information, and I don't think he understood all the information he was releasing. I don't think anyone could have understood it all.

Ellsberg, who worked at the RAND Corporation at the time and had this contract to analyze the Vietnam War, but realized at a point long before the war had ended that [the government] knew they were never going to win it, and realized that this information should be part of the public debate, and decided *in a very self-conscious way* to make this information part of the public debate. Snowden reminded me so much of Ellsberg. Not in his personality, but in the reflective way he decided to be.

If we take the *Guardian* at its word, and we take Snowden at his word, he released information that would not endanger active agents or reveal the location of CIA stations. So I think Ellsberg is an obvious comparison. And I think the significance of all this is going to end up being comparable to the significance of the Pentagon papers.

MJ: Are there personality traits that make someone prone to becoming a whistleblower?

FA: I thought there were when I started to write my book. I thought that's what I was setting out to do. I decided there may be but I don't think I'm going to find it, and I don't think anybody's going to find it. I do think there are certain moral descriptions we can make about whistleblowers, that they tend to be conservative in some ways.

The best way I can describe it: A whistleblower I spoke with whose name will never make the newspaper, he said something like, "I wasn't against the system, I *was* the system! I just didn't realize that there were two systems."

"He said, 'I wasn't against the system, I *was* the system! I just didn't realize that there were two systems.'"

Most of us grow up to realize that what people say and what people do are two things. We learn a certain cynicism about life, like that everything a politician promises isn't necessarily going to be what he does. I think whistleblowers somehow come late to this realization. They're naive in a certain sense, and then when they come to realize that people are lying, cheating, stealing, whatever, they're shocked. It's kind of like, what's that line from *Casablanca?* They're "shocked that gambling's going on in this place"!

Whistleblowers are shocked in a way that the rest of us aren't, and that leads them to act. In a sense, they hardly have a choice. This is what most of them said to me; I don't know what Snowden will say in 5 or 10 years. But the ones I spoke with who had blown the whistle maybe 5, 10 years ago, many of them said they wouldn't do it again, and many of them said they would. All of them said they didn't have a choice. They couldn't live with themselves anymore without doing something.

MJ: So Edward Snowden seems authentic to you?

FA: I mean, how can you know for sure? But as I listen to him, as I look at the *Guardian*'s account, and I look at the background—they paid a lot of time and attention checking out this guy.

What makes him an unusual whistleblower is that he's not just putting his job and his personal happiness on the line, he's putting the rest of his life in jail on the line. I don't think that's likely, but it's certainly possible. Ellsberg was prosecuted, and had Nixon's gang not bungled the burglary at Lewis Fielding's office, Ellsberg could have gone to jail for 20 years.

MJ: Do you think most whistleblowers understand what the long-term consequences of their actions will be? Do you think Edward Snowden did?

FA: Most don't. Most have no idea. Let me put it this way: What you reveal when you talk about immorality or another ethical behavior as organizational policy is that you're somebody who remembers the outside even when you're on the inside. You've given yourself away, and many whistleblowers think they'll be rewarded or they'll be thanked. And if they think, "Well, I'll get fired," they certainly don't understand how their friends at work—many of whom they've spent more time with than their families—will be so scared they won't even look at them. Many of them have no understanding of their years in exile, and the stress it takes on their families.

I get calls and emails from whistleblowers. I tell them, check your finances, check the state of your marriage, to try to give them some idea of what's going to be involved. Usually, they've just become a whistleblower and things have started to go bad. And I try to tell them, "Well, that's normal." They're in for a long, tough road. And unfortunately, what it takes to become a whistleblower—that certain naivete—isn't what it takes to survive as a whistleblower, which is a hard-hearted cynicism.

"What it takes to become a whistleblower—that certain naivete—isn't what it takes to survive as a whistleblower, which is a hard-hearted cynicism."

I think Snowden is different. I think he understands very well.

MJ: I wonder if those sacrifices are as painful for someone with a whistleblower's personality, or if he's more comfortable being alone in the first place.

FA: It hurts. They're all wounded. They really are. Even people who are used to it, it's just like anyone else. Maybe people like this are a little more used to being alone.

MJ: Whistleblowers have a reputation for being egotistical. Why is that?

FA: I think it's more a survival strategy than anything else. I don't think whistleblowers have more ego invested in what they do, or maybe they need it.

They tend to be a little more obsessive than other people. They're not necessarily the person I'd like to have a drink with. You start to go talk to whistleblowers in their homes—now people's old records are more electronic, but even just a few years ago—and their basements or their attics would be filled with troves of file after file after file.

MJ: Do you think it would be possible for an agency or organization to screen out whistleblower-types? There's certainly an incentive to try.

FA: I don't think so. Because if you think about it, they're awfully close to the all-American boy or girl. They're not the zealot, the deviant, the crusader—they may become some of these things later on but they don't enter the organization this way.

MJ: Often whistleblowers are cast as having ulterior motives for doing what they did, like Bradley Manning being driven by gender confusion. What do you think when you see that happening?

FA: The whistleblowers have a name for it: "nuts and sluts." That the response of the organization will be to pathologize the whistleblower: Take the focus off the issue and put the focus on the whistleblower. I think with Bradley Manning, one has to ask the question I've already asked: Whether a large data dump is really the way to go about whistleblowing and what other alternatives where there to him.

MJ: What does Edward Snowden have in store for him in the coming days and months?

FA: People are already talking about his age. I read a column by David Brooks that wasn't entirely damning, but it was already about his social alienation. That this is the consequence of social alienation, where half of him may have some good qualities, but he's socially alienated and doesn't understand his obligation to his fellow citizens as a consequence.

To be a whistleblower, to be a moral human being in this society, probably requires some level of—well, he can call it alienation, I call it not having completely bought into the system. It sounds like Edward Snowden had a pretty good life in Hawaii, he had a girlfriend. He's not like some hermit that crawled out of the woods after 27 years.

It's going to be hard to make [the socially alienated idea] stick if Snowden can keep his presence out there a little bit. Because he doesn't seem like a crazed, alienated zealot.

MJ: When he talked about the government in the *Guardian* video, he seemed suspicious of it, and like he has a very hardline view on privacy issues.

FA: He does. But these are policies that are able to be discussed publicly without compromising the security of the nation. I see the ACLU is already suing to stop some of these data-gathering practices and that's the way they ought to be, and if people don't know about them then they can't stop them. That's the point: They ought to be subject to debate.

What he is absolutely right about, and he said it right out front: Whistleblowing has to be connected to a name and a face to really make a difference, and doing this anonymously is far less effective.

MJ: Why do these stories need a face attached to them?

FA: I don't know. Why do we like to go to the movies? This is a personal story, and we like to tell narratives, and he makes it interesting. Because how many people are going to sit down and read these documents and make sense of them? If attaching his name to it somehow keeps the story alive, it's too bad, but that's the way it is.

Opting to Blow the Whistle or Choosing to Walk Away

By Alina Tugend
The New York Times, September 20, 2013

Whistleblowers have been big news lately—from Chelsea Manning, formerly known as Pfc. Bradley Manning, to Edward J. Snowden. Yet, for most people, the question of whether to expose unethical or illegal activities at work doesn't make headlines or involve state secrets.

But that doesn't make the problem less of a quandary. The question of when to remain quiet and when to speak out—and how to do it—can be extraordinarily difficult no matter what the situation.

And while many think of ethics violations as confined to obviously illegal acts, like financial fraud or safety violations, the line often can be much blurrier and, therefore, more difficult to navigate.

According to the Ethics Resource Center, a nonprofit research organization, the No. 1 misconduct observed—by a third of 4,800 respondents—was misuse of company time. That was closely followed by abusive behavior and lying to employees.

The findings were published in the organization's 2011 National Business Ethics Survey, which interviewed, on the phone or online, employees in the commercial sector who were employed at least 20 hours a week. It has been conducted biannually since 1994.

But offensive behavior that creates a hostile work environment, although often not thought of as unethical behavior, is the leading reason people leave their jobs, said Patricia J. Harned, president of the center. "Abusive and intimidating behavior by supervisors and managers creates a toxic work environment."

So does lying to employees. Lester, who asked that I use only his first name to avoid possible legal issues, worked at a global consulting company for about three years, earning high performance ratings. At one point, he said, he accidentally learned that his manager had deliberately lied to deny him a promotion opportunity. Lester spoke to the hiring manager to no avail, and because the company had a strong ethics program — including a specific "no retaliation policy" and a hot line to report ethics complaints — he reported the situation.

An investigation found no wrongdoing, and although Lester appealed the findings, no action was taken against the manager. That is when he says the retaliation began.

"All my direct reports were taken away from me and I was given the most difficult projects with the least resources," he said. "A whole series of things happened, which were unlikely to be a coincidence."

After about eight months of this, he decided to leave.

Lester's experience may be the reason the misconduct most often seen is not the one most often reported. According to the Ethics Resources Center report, which is sponsored by major corporations like Wal-Mart and Northrop Grumman, less than half of those who observed a boss lying to employees reported it.

On the other hand, while only 12 percent said they had witnessed someone stealing from the company, almost 70 percent of those who saw such activity reported it.

One of the difficulties in cases like Lester's is that no law has been broken. True whistleblowing, according to Stephen M. Kohn, a lawyer and executive director of the National Whistleblowers Center, is when people report seeing or experiencing something at their company that is against the law, rather than cases in which employees feel mistreated, but nothing illegal has occurred.

It appears, however, that an increasing number of employees are willing to come forward in both types of cases. More people are using their companies' ethics procedures to report misconduct, and more people are filing whistleblower claims.

Mr. Kohn, whose organization refers potential whistleblowers to lawyers, said there had been a 30 percent increase in the number of people requesting referrals over the last 18 months, which comes to about 1,500 requests a year.

He also said the quality of complaints—with more documentation and from higher-level employees—had increased.

Some of this is because of legislation rewarding whistleblowers for coming forth and protecting them against retaliation. The most prominent of those is the Dodd-Frank Act, which passed in 2010. Under that act, the Securities and Exchange Commission oversees the Office of the Whistleblower, which in 2012 alone received 3,001 tips.

It may seem counterintuitive that reporting bad behavior would go up during the recession and afterward, when people fear for their jobs. Ms. Harned said, however, that one explanation was that employees were less able to change jobs, so they might be more willing to try to change a negative work culture.

"Historically, when the economy is good, companies take more risks and focus more on the bottom line," Ms. Harned said. "They're not talking about ethics as much."

But, just as reporting is on the rise, so is retaliation. More than one in five employees interviewed said they experienced some sort of reprisal when they reported misconduct, ranging from being excluded from decision-making activities and getting the cold shoulder from other employees to being passed over for promotion.

That is almost double the number who said they were retaliated against in the 2007 study.

Even more alarming, in 2009, 4 percent of those who said they experienced reprisals for reporting wrongdoing cited physical threats to themselves or their property. In 2011, that rose to 31 percent.

"Whistleblowing does threaten cultures and individuals, even when companies say they want it and think they want it," said Kirk O. Hanson, executive director of the Markkula Center for Applied Ethics at Santa Clara University.

And, he said, it's very easy to rationalize that an action—say, denying a promotion—is not actually payback for reporting misconduct, but because the worker isn't a team player.

So, while it's important to expose unethical behavior, it's also necessary to be very clear why you're doing it—and how to do it right.

"A good thing to ask yourself is, 'Why am I doing this? Am I trying to help the company or just get someone in trouble?'" said Stuart Sidle, director of the Industrial-Organizational Psychology program at the University of New Haven.

You need to ensure that you're not talking yourself out of taking an ethical stand, nor talking yourself into reporting something for the wrong reason, Professor Hanson said.

"Have someone you can bounce dilemmas off who has similar values," he said. "To make sure you're not rationalizing not doing anything, and to make sure there's a genuine problem—someone to help you be strong but also to test your realities."

In general, employees should follow the proper channels, like addressing the issue with the person directly supervising the supposed culprit, said John M. Thornton, a professor of accounting ethics at Azusa Pacific University.

Along the same lines, think very hard before going public.

"I question someone trying to report externally before reporting internally," Mr. Sidle said. It's too easy, now, he said, to put up a video of bad behavior on YouTube or lash out on Facebook without ever speaking with the people who might be willing to resolve the problems.

On the other hand, don't shy away from reporting bad behavior because you don't want to be seen as that worst elementary school insult—a tattletale.

"You don't want a culture of tattling, but you do want a culture of telling if something is harming the company and the community," Professor Sidle said.

And companies need to be specific in how they talk about ethics, he added.

"It's useless just to talk about unethical behavior," he said. "Everyone is against fraud. Everyone is against disrespectful behavior, but how is it defined? Leadership has to give examples. If someone asks you to backdate something because the client asked, it's unethical, even if it's commonly done."

And, finally, whistleblowers should know that most cases are not settled in their favor. "This may be attributable to injustices in the system, or lack of merit or proof of the alleged wrongdoing," Professor Thornton said.

For good or for bad, most of us will never face the decisions that Mr. Manning and Mr. Snowden have. But that doesn't mean our choices—to confront or to ignore—aren't important.

"Some will always cheat on their expense reports," Professor Hanson said. "Some will never cheat. Most of us are in the middle. It's a constant struggle to do the right thing."

Survey Shows Increase in Whistleblowers Reporting Misconduct, but in Retaliation as Well

By Hannah Johnson
Government Accountability Project, June 11, 2013

The Ethics Resource Center (ERC)—a research-oriented nonprofit aimed at promoting high ethical standards in business—released its 2011 *National Business Ethics Survey* (NBES) report recently.

Turns out the past couple years have been a pretty mixed bag for whistleblowers. So . . . good news or bad news first?

Let's start with the good news. The percentage of corporate employees surveyed who said they've *seen* misconduct at work fell to just 45 percent, compared to 49 percent in 2009 and a record high of 55 percent in 2007. On the flip side, the number of those who are *reporting* that misconduct at work is at a record high – 65 percent. This is up an impressive 12 points from 2005 (53 percent).

This is an uplifting trend. Employees are witnessing less misconduct at work, but when it happens, it is [they are] more likely to report it. This is one of the most effective ways to ensure the misconduct levels stay low.

Now for the bad news. The ERC also reports "ominous warning signs of a potentially significant ethics decline ahead." Retaliation against employees who reported misconduct rose 10 points from 2007 to 22 percent. That's more than *one in five* who faced some sort of retaliation for their disclosure. In addition, 42 percent of companies are reported to have weak ethics cultures, a steep rise from 35 percent two years ago. More employees (13 percent) are feeling pressure to compromise their ethical standards since 2000.

The ERC says these two rather opposing trends are unlike any previous patterns in past years' reports. The organization identifies the economy and increased social networking as two of the driving forces behind them. How? Well, misconduct being down and reporting of it being up is occurring while many are still anxious about the possibility of a second recession – Americans are still all too aware of the long term effects of corporate misconduct. And employees who are active social networkers experience much higher pressure to conform to misconduct and face higher retaliation rates.

As the Project on Government Oversight explained in a recent blog post, a supplement to this study, *Inside the Mind of the Whistleblower*, seems to disprove the argument Rep. Michael Grimm (R-NY) makes for stripping financial whistleblower protections: that whistleblowers will start to report solely outside the company for a financial reward, not giving companies the opportunity to supposedly act properly and correct their mistakes. In reality, the survey shows, only 2 percent would report outside the company first, and about one in 20 said they were motivated by financial reward.

But it seems whistleblowers are in good company, with a majority of those who witness misconduct choosing to report it. The more information available to employees about their rights and blowing the whistle, the more employees will be willing to step forward. In fact, this has been one of the main goals of GAP's successful *American Whistleblower Tour*—educating our youth about how whistleblowers make a difference, and what their rights are.

The Whistleblower's Quandary

By Adam Waytz, James Dungan, and Liane Young
The New York Times, August 2, 2013

Imagine you're thinking about blowing the whistle on your employer. As the impassioned responses to the actions of whistleblowers like Edward J. Snowden have reminded us, you face a moral quandary: Is reporting misdeeds an act of heroism or betrayal?

In a series of studies, we investigated how would-be whistleblowers make this decision. Our findings, to be published in the *Journal of Experimental Social Psychology*, not only shed light on the moral psychology of whistleblowing but also reveal ways to encourage or discourage the practice.

In one study, we asked a group of 74 research participants to write a paragraph about an occasion when they witnessed unethical behavior and reported it (and why), and we asked another group, of 61 participants, to write about an occasion when they witnessed unethical behavior and kept their mouths shut. We found that the whistleblowers used 10 times as many terms related to *fairness* and *justice,* whereas non-whistleblowers used twice as many terms related to *loyalty.*

It makes sense that whistleblowing brings these two moral values, fairness and loyalty, into conflict. Doing what is fair or just (e.g., promoting an employee based on talent alone) often conflicts with showing loyalty (e.g., promoting a longstanding but unskilled employee).

Although fairness and loyalty are both basic moral values, some people prioritize one over the other. Studies show that American liberals tend to focus more on fairness, while American conservatives tend to focus more on loyalty, which may help explain differing responses to Mr. Snowden. To some he was defending the rights of all Americans; to others he was a traitor to his country.

Does such variation in moral values predict whether someone will decide to blow the whistle? In another study, we gave 83 research participants a questionnaire. Some questions probed their concern for fairness (e.g., "whether or not someone was denied his or her rights"), whereas others probed their concern for loyalty (e.g., "whether or not someone did something to betray his or her group"). We computed a "fairness score" and a "loyalty score" for each participant. We also asked questions about how likely they would be to report a stranger, an acquaintance, a friend and a family member for crimes of varying severity (from petty theft to murder).

We found that neither fairness nor loyalty alone predicted whistleblowing. However, the way people traded one value against another—the difference between people's fairness and loyalty scores—did. People who valued fairness more than loyalty expressed greater willingness to blow the whistle, whereas people who valued loyalty more than fairness were more hesitant.

To test whether such whistleblowing decisions are susceptible to manipulation, we asked 293 participants across two experiments about their willingness to blow the whistle, but first we had them write short essays on the importance of fairness or the importance of loyalty. We compared whistleblowing scores between these two groups and found that participants who wrote about fairness were more willing to blow the whistle than those who wrote about loyalty.

In our final study, we sought to determine whether this writing exercise could be used to influence people's behavior in a nonhypothetical situation. For our real-world test, we focused on Amazon's Mechanical Turk, an online marketplace where users ("requesters") post tasks like proofreading and evaluating advertisements, to be completed by other users ("workers") in exchange for money. Reputation is paramount on Mechanical Turk, and users can publicly evaluate and even blacklist one another.

In our study, involving 142 users of Mechanical Turk, we first asked the participants to write a short essay about the importance of fairness or loyalty. Then we made sure that all of the participants at some point during the study witnessed the substandard work of a fellow Mechanical Turk user. At the end of the study, we surprised the participants by creating a whistleblowing quandary: we asked whether the user whose shoddy work they witnessed had violated any rules and whether we should block that user from future tasks. When we compared the responses from our two groups, we found that those who had written about the importance of fairness were significantly more willing to report a fellow worker than those who had written about loyalty. Even a nudge can affect people's whistleblowing behavior.

This does not mean that a five-minute writing task will cause government contractors to leak confidential information. But our studies suggest that if, for instance, you want to encourage whistle-blowing, you might emphasize fairness in mission statements, codes of ethics, honor codes or even ad campaigns. And to sway those who prize loyalty at all costs, you could reframe whistle-blowing, as many have done in discussing Mr. Snowden's case, as an act of "larger loyalty" to the greater good. In this way, our moral values need not conflict.

Why You Should Applaud Dissent, Not Fire It

By Jeremy Quittner
Inc., September 19, 2014

Startups and small businesses have a lot of things going for them, namely, their potential to be open, to foster constructive dissent and to use different ideas to spark innovation.

I thought about those things when I listened to the powerful segment produced by *Propublica* and *This American Life* about whistleblower Carmen Segarra, whose 46 hours of secret taping at the Federal Reserve Bank of New York and Goldman Sachs sheds light on the failings of corporate cultures that squelch dissent. Segarra's tapes are being called the "Ray Rice video" of the financial sector.

And they're particularly important because the Federal Reserve Bank of New York perhaps had a greater role in the financial crisis than any other in its federation, due to its oversight of the big Wall Street banks, including Lehman Brothers, the anniversary of whose collapse was September 15.

Segarra, who speaks four languages and has degrees from Cornell, Harvard, and the Sorbonne, was hired in 2011 by the Federal Reserve Bank of New York to help regulate one of the largest investment banks in the world, Goldman Sachs. Her role was to ask questions and look for problems similar to those at a host of prominent banks that led to the crippling of the financial system in 2008.

But Segarra soon butted up against the culture of the New York Fed, which has been criticized for being uncomfortably cozy with the banks it's chartered to oversee. Those problems were first identified by Columbia University finance professor, David Beim, who was invited in by the New York Fed to analyze the shortcomings that led to the crisis. In a lengthy report to the bank in 2009, Beim identified a culture where regulators were afraid to speak up and to contradict bosses.

A Culture Trap

Beim's observations about the Federal Reserve Bank of New York's failing are almost like a checklist for small business owners who wants to make sure their own culture isn't falling into a similar trap. Among the reserve bank's problems:

- An employee reluctance to be too far outside of what managers are thinking.
- An organization that does not encourage thinking outside the box.

- A reluctance to bring up ideas once they have been shot down a couple of times.
- Not speaking up until people know what their bosses are thinking.

When Segarra tried to push back against the culture, in particular by identifying what she thought were irregularities in Goldman's deal-making, as well as its nearly non-existent conflict of interest policy, she was shutdown and eventually fired.

And firing an employee for speaking up should be anathema to small business owners, entrepreneurship experts say.

"In all of my startup classes, I teach the value of dissent," says Mitchell Fillet, a professor of finance and entrepreneurship at Fordham University, in New York. "If everyone agrees with you, you are probably not doing something right, because nobody is perfect, and you need someone to point out that something is wrong."

Yet the role of the dissenter is often an uncomfortable one, and the dissenter is often punished, Fillet says. He points to Steve Jobs, who was pushed out by Apple's board in the mid-1980s, as an example. Jobs was known for his temper, but also his perfectionism and his fearlessness about speaking his own mind.

Diversity Works

At the same time, some of the most successful companies today emphasize openness to different points of view from employees and customers alike, says Caroline Daniels, a professor of entrepreneurship at Babson College. And that allows companies to innovate more quickly, and to pivot into directions that can help them be more successful.

In that regard, I thought of Google's efforts to diversify its workforce, because it realizes that having an employee base that's 83 percent white and male is a liability for developing critical new ideas and to its own creativity.

It's a lesson for all small business owners to keep in mind: value and encourage different viewpoints.

"Once you hear a CEO say, 'Let's stay within our strategic avenue for innovation,' you know that innovation is in trouble," Daniels says.

The Banality of Systemic Evil

By Peter Ludlow
The New York Times, September 15, 2013

In recent months there has been a visible struggle in the media to come to grips with the leaking, whistleblowing and hacktivism that has vexed the United States military and the private and government intelligence communities. This response has run the gamut. It has involved attempts to condemn, support, demonize, psychoanalyze and in some cases canonize figures like Aaron Swartz, Jeremy Hammond, Chelsea Manning and Edward Snowden.

In broad terms, commentators in the mainstream and corporate media have tended to assume that all of these actors needed to be brought to justice, while independent players on the Internet and elsewhere have been much more supportive. Tellingly, a recent *Time* magazine cover story has pointed out a marked generational difference in how people view these matters: 70 percent of those age 18 to 34 sampled in a poll said they believed that Snowden "did a good thing" in leaking the news of the National Security Agency's surveillance program.

So has the younger generation lost its moral compass?

No. In my view, just the opposite.

Clearly, there is a moral principle at work in the actions of the leakers, whistleblowers and hacktivists and those who support them. I would also argue that that moral principle has been clearly articulated, and it may just save us from a dystopian future.

In *Eichmann in Jerusalem*, one of the most poignant and important works of 20th-century philosophy, Hannah Arendt made an observation about what she called "the banality of evil." One interpretation of this holds that it was not an observation about what a regular guy Adolf Eichmann seemed to be, but rather a statement about what happens when people play their "proper" roles within a system, following prescribed conduct with respect to that system, while remaining blind to the moral consequences of what the system was doing—or at least compartmentalizing and ignoring those consequences.

A good illustration of this phenomenon appears in "Moral Mazes," a book by the sociologist Robert Jackall that explored the ethics of decision making within several corporate bureaucracies. In it, Jackall made several observations that dovetailed with those of Arendt. The mid-level managers that he spoke with were not "evil" people in their everyday lives, but in the context of their jobs, they had a separate moral code altogether, what Jackall calls the "fundamental rules of corporate life":

(1) You never go around your boss. (2) You tell your boss what he wants to hear, even when your boss claims that he wants dissenting views. (3) If your boss wants something dropped, you drop it. (4) You are sensitive to your boss's wishes so that you anticipate what he wants; you don't force him, in other words, to act as a boss. (5) Your job is not to report something that your boss does not want reported, but rather to cover it up. You do your job and you keep your mouth shut.

Jackall went through case after case in which managers violated this code and were drummed out of a business (for example, for reporting wrongdoing in the cleanup at the Three Mile Island nuclear power plant).

Aaron Swartz counted *Moral Mazes* among his "very favorite books." Swartz was the Internet wunderkind who was hounded by a government prosecution threatening him with 35 years in jail for illicitly downloading academic journals that were behind a pay wall. Swartz, who committed suicide in January at age 26 (many believe because of his prosecution), said that *Moral Mazes* did an excellent job of "explaining how so many well-intentioned people can end up committing so much evil."

Swartz argued that it was sometimes necessary to break the rules that required obedience to the system in order to avoid systemic evil. In Swartz's case the system was not a corporation but a system for the dissemination of bottled up knowledge that should have been available to all. Swartz engaged in an act of civil disobedience to liberate that knowledge, arguing that "there is no justice in following unjust laws. It's time to come into the light and, in the grand tradition of civil disobedience, declare our opposition to this private theft of public culture."

Chelsea Manning, the United States Army private incarcerated for leaking classified documents from the Departments of Defense and State, felt a similar pull to resist the internal rules of the bureaucracy. In a statement at her trial she described a case where she felt this was necessary. In February 2010, she received a report of an event in which the Iraqi Federal Police had detained 15 people for printing "anti-Iraqi" literature. Upon investigating the matter, Manning discovered that none of the 15 had previous ties to anti-Iraqi actions or suspected terrorist organizations. Manning had the allegedly anti-Iraqi literature translated and found that, contrary to what the federal police had said, the published literature in question "detailed corruption within the cabinet of Prime Minister Nuri Kamal al-Maliki's government and the financial impact of his corruption on the Iraqi people."

When Manning reported this discrepancy to the officer in charge (OIC), she was told to "drop it," she recounted.

Manning could not play along. As she put it, she knew if she "continued to assist the Baghdad Federal Police in identifying the political opponents of Prime Minister al-Maliki, those people would be arrested and in the custody of the Special Unit of the Baghdad Federal Police and very likely tortured and not seen again for a very long time—if ever." When her superiors would not address the problem, she was compelled to pass this information on to WikiLeaks.

Snowden too felt that, confronting what was clearly wrong, he could not play his proper role within the bureaucracy of the intelligence community. As he put it,

> [W]hen you talk to people about [abuses] in a place like this where this is the normal state of business people tend not to take them very seriously and move on from them. But over time that awareness of wrongdoing sort of builds up and you feel compelled to talk about [them]. And the more you talk about [them] the more you're ignored. The more you're told it's not a problem until eventually you realize that these things need to be determined by the public and not by somebody who was simply hired by the government.

The bureaucracy was telling him to shut up and move on (in accord with the five rules in *Moral Mazes*), but Snowden felt that doing so was morally wrong.

In a June Op-Ed in The Times, David Brooks made a case for why he thought Snowden was wrong to leak information about the Prism surveillance program. His reasoning cleanly framed the alternative to the moral code endorsed by Swartz, Manning and Snowden. "For society to function well," he wrote, "there have to be basic levels of trust and cooperation, a respect for institutions and deference to common procedures. By deciding to unilaterally leak secret N.S.A. documents, Snowden has betrayed all of these things."

The complaint is eerily parallel to one from a case discussed in *Moral Mazes*, where an accountant was dismissed because he insisted on reporting "irregular payments, doctored invoices, and shuffling numbers." The complaint against the accountant by the other managers of his company was that "by insisting on his own moral purity . . . he eroded the fundamental trust and understanding that makes cooperative managerial work possible."

But wasn't there arrogance or hubris in Snowden's and Manning's decisions to leak the documents? After all, weren't there established procedures determining what was right further up the organizational chart? Weren't these ethical decisions better left to someone with a higher pay grade? The former United States ambassador to the United Nations, John Bolton, argued that Snowden "thinks he's smarter and has a higher morality than the rest of us . . . that he can see clearer than other 299,999,999 of us, and therefore he can do what he wants. I say that is the worst form of treason."

For the leaker and whistleblower the answer to Bolton is that there can be no expectation that the system will act morally of its own accord. Systems are optimized for their own survival and preventing the system from doing evil may well require breaking with organizational niceties, protocols or laws. It requires stepping outside of one's assigned organizational role. The chief executive is not in a better position to recognize systemic evil than is a middle level manager or, for that matter, an IT contractor. Recognizing systemic evil does not require rank or intelligence, just honesty of vision.

Persons of conscience who step outside their assigned organizational roles are not new. There are many famous earlier examples, including Daniel Ellsberg (the Pentagon Papers), John Kiriakou (of the Central Intelligence Agency) and several former N.S.A. employees, who blew the whistle on what they saw as an unconstitutional and immoral surveillance program (William Binney, Russ Tice and Thomas Drake, for example). But it seems that we are witnessing a new generation of whistleblowers and leakers, which we might call generation W (for the generation that came of age in the era WikiLeaks, and now the war on whistleblowing).

The media's desire to psychoanalyze members of generation W is natural enough. They want to know why these people are acting in a way that they, members of the corporate media, would not. But sauce for the goose is sauce for the gander; if there are psychological motivations for whistleblowing, leaking and hacktivism, there are likewise psychological motivations for closing ranks with the power structure within a system — in this case a system in which corporate media plays an important role. Similarly it is possible that the system itself is sick, even though the actors within the organization are behaving in accord with organizational etiquette and respecting the internal bonds of trust.

Just as Hannah Arendt saw that the combined action of loyal managers can give rise to unspeakable systemic evil, so too generation W has seen that complicity within the surveillance state can give rise to evil as well — not the horrific evil that Eichmann's bureaucratic efficiency brought us, but still an Orwellian future that must be avoided at all costs.

Whistleblowing Is Coming Soon to a Private-Sector Company Near You

By Shel Holtz
Holz Communication + Technology, September 13, 2013

Back in 2006, Michael De Kort was a Lockheed Martin engineer working on a Coast Guard contract when he became increasingly convinced that the work his employer was doing left the ships vulnerable to attack. According to De Kort, blind spots in the vessel's surveillance system would expose the crew, the communications system was vulnerable to eavesdropping, and some of the equipment wouldn't be able withstand extreme cold temperatures.

De Kort tried to get people to listen to his concerns, contacting everyone from his bosses to government investigators to congressmen. Unable to get anyone to pay attention, he finally resorted to posting his concerns in the form of a 10-minute YouTube video. Shortly afterwards, he was laid off.

De Kort's story got some coverage (like this *Washington Post* piece), and in 2008 he was recognized for his efforts with the Carl Barus Award for Outstanding Service in the Public Interest from the IEEE Society. He is listed in the *Online Ethics Center for Engineering and Research*. But little about his experience would inspire others to blow the whistle on unethical practices.

In fact, whistleblowers usually don't end up well. Efforts to improve outcomes for whistleblowers have been stymied at every turn. What seemed like a positive step by the U.S. Senate in approving the Whistleblower Protection Act by unanimous consent turned into just another roadblock when a senator placed an anonymous secret hold on the law, which would have allowed federal workers to report government corruption.

Things are changing for whistleblowers these days, though. Edward Snowden is the latest whistleblower to have the lights of both mainstream and social media shined upon him. While he is being vilified as a traitor by some, others proclaim him a hero. It's a pattern we have seen with Bradley Manning and Julian Assange.

I am taking no position in this article on the rightness or wrongness of Snowden, Manning and Assange's actions. But whatever other motives may have driven them, each has spoken openly of their inability to do nothing in the face of what they perceived to be outrageous ethical violations. Whether or not you're inclined to believe them, all three belong to a generation that places a higher value on ethics and, as a result, may be willing to risk more in order to do what they believe to be the right thing.

2010 study by the Ethics Resource Center found that 12% of Millennials believe it's appropriate to post negative comments about their employers on social sites, while 19% said it's okay to keep copies of confidential documents. In both cases, those numbers are higher than among Gen Xers and Baby Boomers. "This research is an important heads-up for employers," Raytheon's vice president for business ethics and compliance, Patricia Ellis, said at the time. Sandra Evacrs-Manly, VP for corporate responsibility at Northrop Grumman, added, "These findings are leading indicators that are telling us, as employers, to adjust our training and ethics messages to help younger employees handle misconduct."

(Interestingly, the Millennials' premium on ethics doesn't extend to the notion of the "work ethic," according to a Pew Research report; even Millennials find that the work ethic is stronger in older generations.)

A more recent study from The Intelligence Group found that Millennials develop respect for brands based on the ethics, practices and image exhibited by the brand, not from promotion of product attributes. The study's conclusion was characterized by a quote from a respondent, who said, "When I disagree with a brand's ethics, I seek out their competitors, or alternatives to their product or service."

With Millennials an increasing force in the workplace, businesses would be foolhardy to ignore the increased emphasis on ethics. Inevitably, the kind of whistleblowing that has recently been focused on government practices will find its way back into the private sector, with ethically-conflicted workers deciding their values are more important than their jobs and exposing wrongdoing (or, at least, what they believe is wrongdoing). Unauthorized disclosures like Michael De Kort's are likely to become commonplace. And don't ignore the impact of Snowden's revelations on Booz Allen, the contractor that employed him; their stock has lost about 4% of its value since Snowden leaked secret documents (although some doubt the company will suffer long-term repercussions).

There are several things businesses need to do to prepare for the inevitable surge in private-sector whistleblowing. The first should be obvious: Don't engage in the kind of behavior that would make someone want to blow the whistle.

Of course, the larger the company the harder it is for senior leadership to be aware of every activity taking place in the organization. Leaders who sincerely believe the company abides by its values can still be surprised to find bad behavior occurring at lower levels. Companies should begin work now to establish procedures for addressing employee whistleblowers. These steps need to ensure the employee is treated fairly and his or her allegations given an honest review.

Processes should be implemented and communicated that give employees an internal avenue for raising their concerns. Ombudsman programs have been effective where they have been implemented based on a sincere and authentic desire to root out unethical practices. Whatever process the organization settles on, it should satisfy employees that the company means what it says about stopping corruption, shortcuts and other unethical practices, and about how the employees who expose these practices will be treated.

Organizations that have not yet undertaken transparency audits need to get cracking. The more transparent the company is, the less likely it is that there will be anything for disgruntled employees to expose. Better internal communications can also help employees understand the context of their work. Comprehending the big picture can help employees avoid developing misperceptions.

Snowden, Manning and Assange are the tip of the iceberg. I don't want to minimize it by labeling it as "fashionable," but whistleblowers are more popular today than ever. Whistleblowing is about to get a lot more common. Is your organization ready to deal with it when it happens?

Tobacco Whistleblower Talks Cigarette Policies

By Carly Noah
The Michigan Daily, October 29, 2014

Jerry Wigand, the former vice president for research and development at Brown & Williamson Tobacco Corporation, caused significant public outrage when he exposed the company's intentional attempt to increase the carcinogenic and addictive components in its cigarettes. Since then, he's traveled the world just to talk about it.

Wigand spoke at the School of Public Health Wednesday afternoon to a crowd of about 100 people, discussing the potential public health impact and controversy surrounding e-cigarettes, the science behind tobacco engineering that promotes addiction and the current state of the tobacco industry in the United States.

Wigand lost his job at Brown & Williamson and received numerous death threats after disclosing the company's secrets. After his dismissal, he assisted the U.S. Federal Drug Association with their investigation of Brown & Williamson. He became nationally known as a tobacco whistleblower after revealing that the company had altered the tobacco content in its cigarettes on the CBS news program *60 Minutes*. This exposé inspired the 1999 movie, *The Insider*.

In 1995, Wigand reached international prominence when he became the tobacco industry's highest-ranking former executive to address public health and smoking issues. Under incredible pressure himself, with even his wife and family members also receiving threats of violence, he informed the public about the industry's poor health and safety practices.

When discussing his decision to go public with Brown & Williamson's fraudulent practices Wednesday, Wigand stressed the importance of reacting ethically.

"It's a gradual evolution to understand what moral obligations one has with the knowledge they have and to avoid that culpability by being a bystander," he said. "A bystander is someone who watches on and does nothing about it. I had to do something about it."

Wigand recounted how after he went public, Brown & Williamson filed a lawsuit against him because of his public disclosures about the industry's effort to diminish the health and safety issues with tobacco use. The lawsuit was dismissed as a condition in the historic 1996 settlement agreement between the U.S. Attorney General and the tobacco industry.

"Tobacco Whistleblower Talks Cigarette Policies" by Carly Noah. Originally published by The Michigan Daily, October 29, 2014.

Currently, Wigand spends his time in lectures around the world advocating for employees of morally corrupt companies to not stand by idly. He is still active in ligations in the tobacco industry and is works as consultant on tobacco. He also leads a non-profit organization for kids, Smoke-Free Kids Inc., with which he concentrates his energy educating kids about the tobacco industry.

When asked if he would blow the whistle again, Wigand said his involvement in the process was simply planting the seed of change and that he was generally proud of his actions.

"Never did I expect that there would be success or the belief that it would really make a difference," he said. "The media, my students, my family, law enforcement, justice department—they all made it happen. I was just this substantial catalyst."

The event drew a wide variety of attendees, ranging from current students to international tobacco experts.

Pharmacy student Brad Vincent was inspired to attend the lecture after he watched *The Insider.*

"I'm in the health and tobacco class and we watched the movie *The Insider* last week and it was a great movie, we learned a lot about tobacco and the whole process. I was born in the early '90s so I never got to know what happened," Pittson said.

LSA senior Emily Long said she found the lecture particularly relevant to her field of study.

"I am actually writing a senior thesis on electronic cigarettes so I thought this would be a really interesting piece to come here and learn about someone who has a lot more expertise than I have," Long said.

Jose Monzon, a tobacco researcher from Guatemala, found the lecture to be helpful from an international perspective.

"He's a big figure in the tobacco world. I'm interested to learn about the current trends in how tobacco control is affecting populations nowadays and particularly how to reduce tobacco use in low and middle income countries, such as Guatemala."

2
Confronting Perpetrators

(L-R) Associate Director—Chief of Staff—Legal and Quality Assurance of Greater Los Angeles VA Health Care System, Christian Head; Kathrine Mitchell, Medical Director of the Iraq and Afghanistan Post-Development Center in Phoenix, Arizona, Veterans Affairs Health Care System; and Program Specialist, VA National Health Eligibility Center, Scott Davis testify during a hearing on "VA Whistleblowers: Exposing Inadequate Service Provided to Veterans and Ensuring Appropriate Accountability" before the House Veterans Affairs Committee July 8, 2014, on Capitol Hill in Washington, DC. The hearing was in conjunction with the investigation of veterans who died because of delays in treatment while waiting for care in VA facilities in Phoenix, Arizona. Former Veterans Affairs Secretary Eric Shinseki had resigned from his position as a result of the scandal.

Truth and Consequences

In the 1970s plainclothes police officer Frank Serpico went public with revelations about an entrenched culture of corruption in the New York City police department. Serpico became nationally famous and the subject of a movie that bore his name, starring Al Pacino. Serpico had violated one of the basic tenets of police-force culture: He had informed on his fellow officers. The push-back was extreme: vile insults, threats, the very real danger of actually getting murdered. As extreme as Serpico's case was, this can be the classic paradigm of the whistleblower: There is the revelation of immoral or illegal procedure. And then there is the counter-response— or responses. Often it is not as dramatic as the very real, life-and-death threats that came Frank Serpico's way. But the fallout can be intense: Whistleblowers can lose their jobs, their very livelihoods; they can suffer social and professional ostracization, and in some cases—like Edward Snowden—wind up in exile. For the record, Frank Serpico also did have support within the police force, just as whistleblowers do have allies and sympathizers, as well as legal precedence to aid them. The cost, of course, can still be great.

In the words of Tom Devine and Tarek F. Maassarani, "Going public boosts the risks of whistleblowing." Their sober advice is a reminder of the vast undertaking—and risks—the whistleblower runs. "A public whistleblower should not expect justice," they state bluntly. "The only thing that you can count on is the personal satisfaction that you did the right thing and that you lived your values." It is the awful paradox of whistleblowing: Going public is the very definition of whistleblowing. And going public to expose wrongdoing can be a complicated task indeed. There is also an extensive checklist *before* stepping forward: The potential whistleblower needs to consult with his or her family, preparing them for all eventualities. The whistleblower needs to ensure the charges he or she is making aren't embellished in any way; the assertions need to be accurate and the details absolutely airtight. The whistleblower needs to keep meticulous records. "Be prepared," the Devine and Maassarani advise, "to live with the 'whole record' of your life. Any personal vulnerability or peccadillo you possess can, and most likely will, be used against you by your employer." It takes a certain constitution to be able to withstand this sort of scrutiny.

The whistleblower should not always necessarily expect public sympathy, either. As reported by Eyal Press in the *New York Review of Books*: "According to the sociologist Claude Fischer, comparative surveys in subsequent years have consistently shown that US citizens are 'much more likely than Europeans to say that employees should follow a boss's orders even if the boss is wrong'; more likely 'to defer to church leaders and to insist on abiding by the law'; and more likely 'to believe that individuals should go along and get along.'" The public whistleblower should never expect justice in a court of law or in the court of public opinion.

High-profile whistleblowers like Edward Snowden have not—to say the least—received universal public acclaim. The late Peter Drucker, who contributed a groundbreaking erudition to the study of management and business, took quite a dim view of whistleblowing: "Today's 'ethics of organization' debate pays great attention to the duty to be a 'whistle-blower' against retaliation or suppression by his boss or by his organization," Drucker opined in his famous essay "What is 'Business Ethics'?" Calling whistleblowing "ethically quite ambiguous," Drucker went on to link whistleblowers to informants and then made this sweeping claim: "And perhaps it is not quite irrelevant that the only societies in Western history that encouraged informers were bloody and infamous tyrannies—Tiberius and Nero in Rome, the Inquisition in the Spain of Philip II, the French Terror, and Stalin. It may also be no accident that Mao, when he tried to establish dictatorship in China, organized 'whistle-blowing' on a massive scale. For under 'whistle-blowing,' under the regime of the 'informer,' no mutual trust, no interdependencies, and no ethics are possible." Drucker's thesis is, to say the least, blunt: It is the worldview of the whistleblower as snitch, as informant—the agent of state tyranny. Drucker expended a great deal of intellectual energy formulating criteria for the ethical, workable business model. The whistleblower, to him, had no place in any organization—or society—whatsoever.

The Drucker viewpoint—shared by many—is that whistleblowing is, in and of itself, intrinsically wrong and actions taken against whistleblowers are an ideological necessity. "The punishment mounted against ethical resisters is no casual matter. While it may seem to take the form of personal revenge by superiors, retaliation is, in fact, part of a rational and planned process initiated by an organization to destroy the resister's credibility as a witness." (Myron Peretz Glazer and Penina Migdal Glazer) In other words, there is an array of forces who view whistleblowing as intrinsically toxic.

When one throws gender into the mix, the hostility against whistleblowers can become all the more virulent, with the female whistleblower facing extra animus. "As more women are climbing the corporate ladders"—and governmental ladders—"and become part of the executive leadership," Professor Linda Hunt has written, "we are seeing more women in whistleblower situations. As we observe more women in these roles, their decision making and ethics are being scrutinized." Hunt goes on to report that despite recent advancements, women are governed by strictures that simply don't exist in a male context. For one, women are still relatively new to the power structure and must often operate without the benefit of an entrenched support network. Women climbing the corporate ladder are denied the benefit of a supportive circle of associates—which is usually the exclusive province of men. As the perpetual outsider, the female whistleblower can have much less to risk. But the unfortunate consequence of this, however, can be that it "is harder for a woman once brought down, to ever climb the corporate ladder again. Emotionally women do not rebound as easily as their male counterparts."

The case of Jan Kemp presents a telling example of what can befall a female whistleblower. Unlike many examples of whistleblowing depicted in the media, this case was set not in the upper echelons of the corporate world or in the cloak-and-dagger milieu of national security, but in college sports. As cited by CNN, Kemp "in the early 1980s exposed the University of Georgia for allowing football players who failed a remedial English class to play in a bowl game . . . 'There is no real sound academic reason for their being here other than to be utilized to produce income,'" Kemp stated. The repercussions were severe: "She was demoted and then fired, and the trauma led her to attempt suicide twice in the 1980s. She also sued UGA officials, saying she was terminated unlawfully, and won compensatory and punitive damages from a jury. She was later reinstated at the university, and Georgia later tightened academic standards for its athletes."

Clearly there must be incentives to override the forbidding obstacles and consequences potential whistleblowers face. There can be the simple, sincere satisfaction of doing the right thing, of telling the truth—and of stopping the damage. Often the whistleblower, in the words of Eyal Press, "evokes the image of an intrepid truth-teller who sounds the alarm from inside an organization, often at great personal risk, in order to safeguard the public interest." There are vast swaths of the American public who are adamantly hostile to the very idea of the whistleblower, but there are also segments of the population who are "able to see whistleblowers in a positive light and as heroes because of a general cynicism and a lack of trust in government." (Roberta Ann Johnson, *Whistleblowing: When It Works—And Why*)

There is a network of legal protection for whistleblowers, most notably the federally mandated False Claims Act, the bedrock of which is the *qui tam* provision. *Qui tam*, in the lexicon of whistleblowing, is a central concept: The "provision that allows individuals who have knowledge that a corporation or organization is defrauding the government to 'blow the whistle' on the illegal activity." (Morgan & Morgan law firm Web site) The fact that *qui tam* has the sanction of the federal government is, of course, hugely significant. The provisions of the False Claims Act had become relatively toothless, Devine and Maassarani relate, "but by 1986 renewed interest in the prevention of fraud and waste . . . led to an amendment that put the teeth back into" this law that dated back to the Lincoln administration. "Deputizing whistleblowers to file antifraud lawsuits has become the most effective anticorruption measure in our nation's history. In 1985, before the law was modernized, the Justice Department recovered $26 million in civil fraud recoveries—a good year compared with the usual $6 million to $9 million total. Recoveries in the next 21 years totaled nearly $24 billion." Twenty-four billion dollars over two decades buys a lot of encouragement on the part of the federal government. There is also, on a state level, many legal statutes that protect whistleblowers, adapted by most state governments.

In addition, "[f]our major federal laws," Stephen Martin Kohn writes, "provide for the payments of rewards to whistleblowers who can prove that their employers committed fraud. These rewards can be huge." This, of course, leads some whistleblowers open to the charge of simply being interested in lining their own pockets. There are also the many caveats: "Getting a cash reward from the IRS is like playing the Powerball lottery. Very few have yet to score, in part due to a byzantine bureaucracy," and in part because claims can take many years to pay out. (Lynnley Browning, *Newsweek*, January 30, 2104)

In cases of whistleblowing, there is no automatic guarantee of monetary compensation or vindication. The risks and the fallout may or may not be worth it. Blowing the whistle is a complicated, unpredictable endeavor. Whistleblowing, for a variety of reasons, has been on the increase, and with the Web and the massive, ongoing expansion of social media, it is easier and easier to transmit claims of wrongdoing. Yet it is still, in essence, a confusing field, with conflicting public attitudes and the lack of codified legal framework. One can only hope that with time the confusion will fade and a solid, equitable plan of action will come into the fore.

Bibliography

Bernstein, Jake. "Inside the New York Fed: Secret Recordings and a Culture Clash." *Fortune*. September 26, 2014; http://fortune.com/author/jake-bernstein/

Browning, Lynnley. "The Perks of Being a Whistleblower." *Newsweek,* January 30, 2014.

Devine, Tom, and Tarek F. Maassarani. *The Corporate Whistleblower's Survival Guide* (San Francisco: Berrett-Koehler, 2011).

Drucker, Peter. "What Is 'Business Ethics'?" *National Affairs*, spring 1981; http://www.nationalaffairs.com/public_interest/detail/what-is-business-ethics

"Filing a Qui Tam Lawsuit." *Morgan & Morgan* Web site; https://www.whistleblowerattorneys.com/qui-tam-lawsuits

Ganim, Sara. "Women Who Blew Whistle in Student-Athlete Cases and What Happened Next." *CNN*, January 9, 2014; http://www.cnn.com/2014/01/09/us/ncaa-athlete-literacy-whistle-blowers/index.html

Glazer, Myron Peretz, and Penina Migdal Glazer. *The Whistleblowers: Exposing Corruption in Government and Industry* (New York: Basic Books, 1989).

Hunt, Linda. "The Challenges Women Whistleblowers Face." *International Business Research*, April 2010

Johnson, Roberta Ann. *Whistleblowing: When It Works—And Why* (Boulder, CO: Lynne Rienner Publications, 2003).

Kohn, Stephen Martin. "Rewards Give Whistleblowers a Motivation to Reveal Wrongdoing." In Berlatsky, Noah, ed., *Whistleblowers* (Farmington Hills, MI: Greenhaven Press, 2012).

Press, Eyal. "Whistleblower, Leaker, Traitor, Spy." *New York Review of Books,* August 5, 2013; http://www.nybooks.com/blogs/nyrblog/2013/aug/05/whistleblower-leaker-traitor-spy/

Don't Shoot the Messenger

By Vanessa Baird
The New Internationalist, April 1, 2014

Is this the age of the whistleblower?

It would seem so, from the column inches, air time and cyberspace given to Edward Snowden.

According to campaigners, the 29-year-old former systems analyst at the US National Security Agency (NSA) is close to being the perfect whistleblower.

A quick look at the video clip interview with Laura Poitras shows why. Measured, thoughtful, Snowden comes across as your average guy, intelligent but with no political axe to grind. He just thinks we should know that the secret services are capturing and storing every phone call we make or internet message we send and that our privacy is being violated wholesale. And he thinks we should at least debate whether we are happy with that or not.

His modest demeanour, his very ordinariness, is in sharp contrast to the scale and impact of his revelations. The sheer amount of data he was able to pass on to select media—some 1.7 million files—beats Chelsea Manning's impressive 251,287 diplomatic cables into a hat.

Since the advent of Wikileaks, whistleblowing has gone from being a "cottage" to an "industrialized" activity, to use the analogy suggested by Icelandic information activist Smári McCarthy.

Yet for most who do it, making disclosures about wrongdoing is a lonely, limiting and isolating affair. It's not like being on a production line with your mates. Paradoxically, this also applies to the most celebrated.

Edward Snowden and Wikileaks founder Julian Assange may have achieved rock-star status but they are fugitives, effectively exiled. Chelsea (formerly Bradley) Manning is serving 35 years in a military jail.

The Obama administration, for all its rhetoric of free speech, has started more prosecutions against whistleblowers than all presidents combined since 1917.

"War against whistleblowers is a toxic trend," says Jesslyn Radack, Snowden's lawyer and a former US Justice Department whistleblower herself.

And not just in the US. Japan recently approved sweeping government powers to punish those who would expose awkward truths about the country's nuclear industry, following the Fukushima disaster.

A Dangerous Vocation

At the source of most exposures of wrongdoing is not a government regulator or police investigator or even an investigative journalist, but a whistleblower. A moral insider who breaks ranks to tell the truth about the malpractice she or he sees.

Once the scandal has broken, such people will be hailed as heroes, admired for their integrity by a public grateful that such courageous and outspoken people exist.

But gratitude offers no protection.

In 2010, millions of Chinese parents were horrified to find that their children were drinking milk that had become mixed with toxic chemicals at fresh milk collection points.

Two years later, one of the two men who exposed the practice, farmer Jiang Weisuo, was murdered in circumstances that have never been explained.

More recent is the case of Lawrence Moepi, a fearless and principled South African auditor, dubbed the "fraudsters' worst nightmare". Last October, as he arrived at his Johannesburg office, he was shot and killed by, it is believed, hired assassins. He had been investigating several suspected corruption cases, including a notorious arms deal.

Silencing or exacting retribution can take many forms, violent and direct—or more devious.

Craig Murray, a former British ambassador who exposed how the British and US secret services were supporting torture in Uzbekistan, was subsequently accused of asking for sex in exchange for visas. It took him 18 months to clear his name.

Janice Karpinsky, the most senior woman in the US army, was arrested and accused of shoplifting the day after revealing that Donald Rumsfeld ordered the torture of prisoners at Abu Ghraib.

Murray comments: "Whistleblowers are rare because it is a near suicidal vocation and everyone else is too scared to help. And if your whistleblowing involves the world of war and spying, they will try to set you up on false charges . . . and not just sack you but destroy you."

While public opinion is generally on the side of whistleblowers, governments, institutions and employers are not. When it comes to the really embarrassing and damaging disclosures, those in power will do all they can to turn the revealer into the enemy.

This has worked on a significant minority of the US public, furious with Manning and Snowden for allegedly putting at risk the security of all Americans. When pressed to say exactly how, the political and secret service players have failed to come up with one concrete example, resorting to vague comments about "agents in the field" and the fact that "terrorists will now change their tactics".

These are high-profile, international cases. But most whistleblowing happens at a far more modest, local level. Sometimes the revelations will reach the local press or emerge during an employment tribunal after the discloser has been dismissed or demoted. Often media outlets are afraid to investigate the information whistleblowers bring them, because they cannot take the risk of a costly libel or defamation suit, or because the story is too complicated or time-consuming to corroborate.

Legal Protection

"Effective whistleblowing arrangements are a key part of good governance," says the British organization Public Concern At Work (PCaW). 'A healthy and open culture is one where people are encouraged to speak out, confident that they can do so without adverse repercussions, confident that they will be listened to, and confident that appropriate action will be taken.'

If only. In the topsy-turvy world of whistleblowing it tends to be the person revealing. wrongdoing, rather than the wrongdoer, who is punished and who ends up losing most—typically their job and career, but often also their relationships, their home, even their liberty.

The complex dynamics at play when someone discloses unwelcome information are explored by psychoanalyst David Morgan in his article "I Had to Do It". Far from being rebels and outsiders, most disclosers are diligent, conscientious, somewhat obsessive insiders, who think their employers will be grateful for the information given and will naturally want to do the right thing.

An increasing number of countries have laws on their statute books—with more in the pipeline—specifically to protect whistleblowers from retaliation, harassment or victimization. But most laws are severely limited in their scope and effectiveness. For example, in Canada and Australia, the law does not apply to people working in the private sector, while New Zealand's law is limited to government agencies.

In Canada, a fierce libel regime contributes to creating possibly the most hostile environment in the English-speaking world. Britain is one of the few European countries with a law that applies across both private and public sectors, but in practice British whistleblowers do not fare too well either and libel laws that favor the rich have a chilling effect. US law is patchy and contradictory, extremely hostile to those who speak out in some areas, but enabling large financial rewards for those who disclose fraud against the government.

While whistleblowers may need to be compensated for loss of earnings, the awarding of massive cash settlements is controversial. Cathy James of the British PCaW sees "moral hazard" in a US-style system. In her view: "Whistleblowing should be seen as a very positive issue, everyone should be encouraged to protect the public interest. I don't want to live in a society where people do the right things because they think they are going to benefit."

Going public on confidential information may put disclosers on the wrong side of the law, especially if they have smuggled out documents or broken official secrecy arrangements. This has led to absurd examples, like that of the banker Bradley Birkenfeld who exposed $780 million tax fraud at UBS, receiving a Swiss prison sentence for breaking confidentiality.

Under British law, disclosers who break the law to reveal wrongdoing can claim, in their defense, that they were acting in the "public interest". This is not widely available elsewhere.

"I Now Recommend Leaking"

Considerable energy goes into lobbying for laws and practices to protect properly those who speak out and many whistleblower organizations believe this is the way forward.

Brian Martin is a veteran campaigner with Whistleblowers Australia who has talked with hundreds of disclosers and written a highly regarded practical guide on the topic.

And he has come to the conclusion that the intense focus on legal protection is misguided.

"It seldom works and can even make whistleblowers more vulnerable; they think they are protected but aren't."

Instead, he now encourages potential disclosers to develop their skills and understanding so that they can be more effective in bringing about change. The most effective strategies, he says, involve taking messages to a wider audience, through mass media, social media or direct communication.

"I now recommend leaking—anonymous whistleblowing—whenever possible."

This may not come naturally to most disclosers, who are conscientious employees who believe the system works. They will try official channels first and are reluctant to contact the media or action groups.

But, Martin points out, whistleblowers are "hardly ever effective in challenging the problems they attempt to expose. This sounds pessimistic. Whistleblowers are courageous but they need a lot of help to be more effective. Probably the best scenario is a link-up between a network of leakers and well-connected action groups."

Smári McCarthy is another activist who is moving away from the legal protection route. For three years he, and others in his native Iceland, worked to create a model legal environment for leakers, whistleblowers and journalists. They were making good headway until April 2013 when a rightwing coalition government came to power and stalled reform.

Now he is focusing more on technology. There are two laws, he says, that governments have to obey: "physics and economics". He plans to use the former to make mass surveillance—whereby intelligence services gather everybody's private internet and phone communication—too expensive to do.

He has calculated that the total budget of the "Five Eyes"—that is the communications snooping services of the US, Britain, Australia, Canada and New Zealand combined – is $120 billion a year. With that they can scoop up the data of 2.5 billion internet users, making the cost per person per day a mere 13 cents.

"My five-year plan is to increase that cost to $10,000 per person per day. The services would have to be a lot more selective and do their job properly."

How to do it? Encryption—the types that hackers have developed and which the NSA has still, as far as we know, not managed to crack. "I use encryption a lot," says McCarthy. "But we need to make it easier to use and available to everyone."

This will help disclosers too, he says, because if everybody's privacy is improved then so is that of whistleblowers. Naturally, their leaks need to be accurate, need to pass the "public interest" test and not gratuitously violate personal privacy.

Snowden and others have revealed the extent to which free speech and civil liberties are being violated by the state, and not just in countries like Russia or China.

More and more information is being classified as top secret and we have no way of debating whether or not it should be. The recent Stasi-style destruction of laptops at *The Guardian* newspaper, under the supervision of Britain's GCHQ, should serve as a warning. As they say, democracy dies behind closed doors—and now too in smashed hard-drives in newspaper offices.

Those genuinely engaged in disclosing in the public interest need protection all along the communication line—from sources and whistleblowers, through campaigners and journalists, to print or web publishers and distributors. In 2011, under a social-democrat government, Iceland followed Council of Europe recommendations and made it illegal for journalists to expose their sources. In Britain a journalist can be jailed for not doing so. It is even worse in the US: Barrett Brown, a young freelancer, is facing 105 years in prison in connection with the posting of information that hackers obtained from Statfor, a private intelligence company with close ties to the federal government.

A Better World

At its heart, whistleblowing is about the desire for truth to be known, for things to be done properly, and for the world to be made a better place.

A place where big business does not cheat or harm citizens for profit, where hospitals and care homes look after frail and elderly people and banks do not rob their customers. Where politicians see office as public service rather than self-service, priests respect the bodily integrity of children in their charge and military personnel do not go on shooting sprees for the hell of it.

Sometimes exposure yields tangible results and the information revealed improves or even saves lives. In 1994, US paralegal Merrell Williams leaked internal memos from Brown & Williamson Tobacco company that showed that the company knew it was lying when it claimed that cigarettes were not harmful, that nicotine was not addictive and that it did not market to children.

His action fueled lawsuits that resulted in an industry pay-out of billions of dollars to pay smokers' medical bills.

Whistleblowers act as the guardians of morality, but too often they are solitary martyrs to democracy. As Wikileaks revealed towards the end of last year, the world is currently facing a major multilateral threat to democracy. It is coming not from religious fanatics in turbans but from fundamentalists in suits.

The acronyms TTP and TTIP are enough to lead even the most committed insomniac to the land of nod. But stay awake, please! This is important. These are US-led international trade deals being negotiated—in conditions of unprecedented secrecy—that will give corporations the power to trump national sovereignty and the interests of billions of people. Two secret drafts of the TransPacific Partnership (TPP), obtained by Wikileaks, on intellectual property and the environment show the deals would trample over individual rights and free expression and give powerful companies the right to challenge domestic laws regulating, for example, resource extraction in Peru or Australia. The Transatlantic Trade and Investment Partnership (TTIP)—between the US and the EU—would have a similar impact, making existing national public services such as health and education even more vulnerable to aggressive action by big private corporations from outside. Those trying to save Britain's national health service from the clutches of private US medical companies know how bad this could be.

Such trade agreements are made at a high level, hatched between a nexus of powerful corporations, governments that do their bidding and secret services that we now know (again, thanks to Snowden) really do use public money to spy on behalf of big business.

The only thing that will counteract the undemocratic and self-serving power of this nexus is a growing network from below that involves whistleblowers, civil society activists and hactivists, journalists and citizens who care.

Only if we have access to information do we have democracy—and today the most relevant information often comes from whistleblowers.

Only if we can participate, is that democracy real—which is why we need to use the information to take action and stop sleepwalking into totalitarianism, be it that of a corrupt institution or a world order devised by and for a global, corporate élite.

Then the tremendous risks that whistleblowers take, and the sacrifices they make, will not be in vain.

Notes

1.   theguardian.com nin.tl/1fCBopA
2.   abc.net.au nin.tl/1hlVQLi
3.   29C3 panel nin.tl/1fCC8Ll
4.   The Ecologist nin.tl/1hlWgkO
5.   craigmurray.org.uk Craig Murray nin.tl/1fCCQbp
6.   Canada's Public Servants Disclosure Act 2000; Australia's Public Interest Disclosure Act 2013
7.   Protected Disclosure Act 2000
8.   Public Interest Disclosure Act 1998
9.   False Claims Act; Dodd-Frank Wall Street Reforms
10.   The Whistleblowing Commission is calling for a mandatory code of practice nin.tl/1hlYaSi
11.   http://pastebin.com/ ahHMhZ1e
12.   Government Accountability Project nin.tl/1fCFTjN
13.   New York Times nin.tl/1hlZ4yn
14.   For example, the Alternative Trade Mandate Network.

Whistleblowers, Beware: Most Claims End in Disappointment, Despair

By Ben Hallman
The Huffington Post, June 4, 2012

At first glance, James Holzrichter's decision to tell the government his employer's dirty secrets appears to have worked out rather well.

He won $6.2 million in 2005 under a federal law, the False Claims Act, that encourages whistleblowers to report fraud against the government. When first contacted by The Huffington Post on Friday, he was on a golf course near his home in Chicago and couldn't talk for long because he was about to play the back nine.

In fact, his decision to sue a former employer, Northrop Grumman, under that federal law cost Holzrichter his profession and nearly two decades of his life.

His court complaint, filed in 1989, languished for years, and so did Holzrichter. He wasn't able to find work as an auditor. He received more than 400 rejection letters from employers who weren't interested, he believes, in hiring a snitch. Desperate to support his wife and four children, he scrubbed toilets and delivered the *Chicago Tribune*. At his lowest moment, he moved his family into a homeless shelter.

"Was it worth it?" Holzrichter said when reached by phone last week, repeating a reporter's question. "I don't know if it was worth it. I have the money, but how can I give my children their childhood back?"

Last year the federal government brought in a record $3 billion from whistleblower cases like Holzrichter's. Not all awards are made public, so it is impossible to provide an exact accounting. But it appears likely that individual whistleblowers received hundreds of millions of dollars from that record haul in bounties for filing the claims that sparked investigations.

This year is shaping up to be even busier than last as the first financial crisis-related cases bear fruit. But would-be whistleblowers, beware. The financial rewards for exposing fraud can be sweet, but the experience is one of uncertainty and despair, and most whistleblowers walk away with no money at all.

"There is a calculated risk in blowing the whistle, but almost no one is telling what those calculations are," said Patrick Burns, a spokesman for Taxpayers Against Fraud, a whistleblower advocacy group.

According to Burns, 80 percent of cases filed under the False Claims Act end with the whistleblower walking away with nothing. Of those who do win a bounty, the average take-home is $150,000. Really big awards are rare, and even then the figures are deceiving. Plaintiffs' lawyers typically claim a major cut, and so does the federal government, in taxes.

Holzrichter said his attorneys received 40 percent of his award, and the government claimed a hefty share in taxes. That left him with $2.3 million—enough to live comfortably on, but in his view, barely fair compensation for 17 years of unemployment and underemployment.

"A lot of people think whistleblowers win the so-called lottery, but they don't understand how much the government and lawyers get," Holzrichter said. "If I had worked until 55 in my profession, I would easily have earned twice that."

There's no data available on how many former company insiders who reported a fraud are unemployed or can't find jobs in their chosen professions, but the anecdotal evidence suggests that many suffer this fate. Holzrichter said he talks to whistleblowers who can't find work, who have health problems and whose marriages are falling apart.

He has helped launch a whistleblower mentoring project so that other company insiders can better understand what they are up against when they report suspected fraud.

In a typical scenario, a whistleblower will file a lawsuit under the False Claims Act, with the hope that the Justice Department will "intervene"—essentially, adopt the case and bring the might of the federal government to bear on the accused wrongdoer.

That's what happened to Kyle Lagow, a former supervisor at LandSafe, a subsidiary of the mortgage giant Countrywide. He sued in 2007 alleging widespread fraud at Countrywide, now part of Bank of America.

Lagow claimed in his lawsuit that Countrywide and mortgage brokers pressured appraisers to falsely inflate values on homes receiving Federal Housing Association–insured loans. Some of those mortgaged homes were underwater from day one.

The Justice Department intervened in his case, and the claims were eventually rolled into what became a $1 billion settlement with Bank of America, announced at the same time as the $25 billion national mortgage settlement reached earlier this year. For his help, Lagow learned in May that he had won $14.5 million.

Lagow, who lives in Plano, Texas, declined through his lawyer to comment for this story. In a Seattlepi.com blog post, the lawyer, Steve Berman, described some of Lagow's struggles.

"Unable to find a job and suffering from cancer, his house went into the foreclosure process," Berman wrote. "His wife and five kids also suffered the punishment for having reported fraud, experiencing poverty and hardship."

Moreover, False Claims Act complaints are filed under seal, which means whistleblowers like Lagow aren't permitted to discuss their cases even with family and friends.

"Kyle went through years of uncertainty in order to see this thing through," said Shayne Stevenson, an attorney who works with Berman and also represented Lagow.

That shouldn't dissuade people with strong cases under the False Claims Act, he said. "The important thing for all whistleblowers to know is that you can be well rewarded," said Stevenson.

And sometimes cases move much faster. Last year, Sherry Hunt, a former vice president in Citigroup's mortgage unit in Missouri, filed a lawsuit claiming that the bank was buying mortgages from outside lenders with doctored tax forms, phony appraisals and missing signatures, and that executives were burying her reports on these defects.

Although Hunt was "ready to give up my career and my life savings to get this done," according to a story in *Bloomberg Markets* magazine, her case sped quickly to its conclusion. Citigroup paid $158 million to settle the lawsuit after Manhattan U.S. Attorney Preet Bharara joined in on behalf of the Justice Department. In February, less than a year after she filed her suit, Hunt won $31 million.

The False Claims Act is not the only means by which federal whistleblowers can seek rewards for their good deeds.

The Internal Revenue Service launched a program focusing on tax fraud in 2006. So far, it has paid a bounty to just one of the dozens of whistleblowers who have come forward.

More promising is a Securities and Exchange Commission program created by the Dodd-Frank financial regulation law. The agency has queued up more than 30 cases that it says are each likely to result in a penalty of more than $1 million— though not necessarily an award.

While most of the SEC cases announced so far deal with smaller-scale fraud, Burns, the whistleblower advocate, said he is optimistic.

"I was extremely skeptical that they would turn around," Burns said. "But the [Bernie] Madoff blast furnace was sufficiently hot on the SEC that it essentially changed the character at the top of the agency, and they never want to be embarrassed like that again."

Why Intelligence Whistleblowers Can't Use Internal Channels

By Conor Friedersdorf
The Atlantic, July 28, 2014

Imagine a CIA agent who witnessed behavior that violated the Constitution, the law, and core human-rights protections, like torturing a prisoner. What would we have her do? Government officials say that there are internal channels in place to protect whistleblowers and that intelligence employees with security clearances have a moral obligation to refrain from airing complaints publicly via the press.

In contrast, whistleblowers like Daniel Ellsberg, Chelsea, Manning and Edward Snowden—as well as journalistic entities like the *Washington Post*, *The Guardian*, and the *New York Times*—believe that questionable behavior by intelligence agencies should sometimes be exposed, even when classified, partly because internal whistleblower channels are demonstrably inadequate.

Reasonable people can disagree about whether a particular leak advances the public interest. There is always a moral obligation to keep some secrets (e.g., the names of undercover agents in North Korea). But if official channels afford little protection to those who report serious wrongdoing, or fail to remedy egregiously unlawful behavior, the case for working within the system rather than going to the press falls apart.[1] As Hilary Bok, writing as Hilzoy, pointed out in 2008, while defending a Bush-era whistleblower:

> It is generally better for all concerned if whistle-blowers operate within the system, and it is dangerous when people freelance. But there's one big exception to this rule: when the system has itself been corrupted. When you're operating within a system in which whistle-blowers' concerns are not addressed—where the likelihood that any complaint you make within the system will be addressed is near zero, while the likelihood that you will be targeted for reprisals is high—then no sane person who is motivated by a desire to have his or her concern addressed will work within that system. That means that if . . . you want whistleblowers to work within the system, you need to ensure that that system actually works.

Today, there is no credible argument that internal channels offer adequate protection to whistleblowers or remedy most serious misdeeds. U.S. officials claim otherwise. They know that no American system of official secrets can be legitimate if it serves to hide behavior that violates the Constitution, the law, or the inalienable rights articulated in the Declaration of Independence.

That they defend the status quo without being laughed out of public life is a testament to public ignorance. Most Americans haven't read the stories of Jesselyn Radack, Thomas Drake, or John Kiriakou; they're unaware of the Espionage Act's sordid history and its unprecedented use by the Obama administration; they don't realize the scale of lawbreaking under President Bush, or that President Obama's failure to prosecute an official torture program actually violates the law; and they're informed by a press that treats officials who get caught lying and misleading (e.g., James Clapper and Keith Alexander) as if they're credible.

Still, every month, more evidence of the national-security state's legitimacy problem comes to light. McClatchy Newspapers reports on the latest illustration that whistleblowers have woefully inadequate protection under current policy and practice:

> The CIA obtained a confidential email to Congress about alleged whistleblower re-taliation related to the Senate's classified report on the agency's harsh interrogation program, triggering fears that the CIA has been intercepting the communications of officials who handle whistleblower cases. The CIA got hold of the legally protected email and other unspecified communications between whistleblower officials and lawmakers this spring, people familiar with the matter told McClatchy. It's unclear how the agency obtained the material.

At the time, the CIA was embroiled in a furious behind-the-scenes battle with the Senate Intelligence Committee over the panel's investigation of the agency's interrogation program, including accusations that the CIA illegally monitored computers used in the five-year probe. The CIA has denied the charges. The email controversy points to holes in the intelligence community's whistleblower protection systems and raises fresh questions about the extent to which intelligence agencies can elude congressional oversight. The email related to allegations that the agency's inspector general, David Buckley, failed to properly investigate CIA retaliation against an agency official who cooperated in the committee's probe, said the knowledgeable people, who asked not to be further identified because of the sensitivity of the matter.

Today's CIA employees have witnessed torturing colleagues in the agency get away with their crimes. They've watched Kiriakou go to jail after objecting to torture. Now, in the unlikely event that they weren't previously aware of it, they've been put on notice that if they engage in whistleblowing through internal channels, during the course of a Senate investigation into past illegal behavior by the CIA, *even then* the protections theoretically owed them are little more than an illusion. Some in Congress have expressed understandable concern. Director of National Intelligence Clapper responded in a letter stating, "the Inspector General of the Intelligence Community . . . is currently examining the potential for internal controls that would ensure whistleblower-related communications remain confidential."

In other words, there aren't adequate safeguards *right now*. This is partly because not enough legislators care about or even know enough to understand the problem. And it is partly because the problem starts right at the top, with Obama and his predecessor. As Marcy Wheeler persuasively argues, the CIA gains significant leverage over the executive branch every time it breaks the law together:

> Torture was authorized by a Presidential Finding—a fact Obama has already gone to extraordinary lengths to hide
>
> CIA has implied that its actions got sanction from that Finding, not the shoddy OLC memos or even the limits placed in those memos, and so the only measure of legality is President Bush's (and the Presidency generally) continued approval of them
>
> CIA helped the (Obama) White House withhold documents implicating the White House from the Senate

Wheeler adds, "This is, I imagine, how Presidential Findings are supposed to work: by implicating both parties in outright crimes, it builds mutual complicity. And Obama's claimed opposition to torture doesn't offer him an out, because within days of his inauguration, CIA was killing civilians in Presidentially authorized drone strikes that clearly violate international law." Obama is similarly implicated in spying that violates the Fourth Amendment. When illegal behavior is endorsed by the president himself, when there is no penalty for blatantly lying to Congress about that behavior, how can internal channels prompt reform?

The public airing of classified information over national-security state objections has been indispensable in bygone instances like the Pentagon Papers, the Church Committee report (back when Congress was doing its job), and the heroic burglary of the COINTELPRO documents. I believe history will judge Manning and Snowden as wrongly persecuted patriots, like Ellsberg. The notion that they should've raised their concerns internally won't be taken seriously, because a dispassionate look at the evidence points to a single conclusion: The United States neither adequately protects whistleblowers nor keeps lawbreaking national-security agencies accountable through internal channels. The next time a leak occurs, the national-security state's defenders should blame themselves for failing to bring about a system that can adequately police itself. If their historical and recent track record weren't so dismal, they'd have a better case to make.

***

¹There is, of course, a sense in which going to the press is "working within the system," if by "the system" one means the Constitution, which guarantees a free press precisely so that the public can get information that the government would rather suppress.

Why Most Financial Whistleblowers Go Unheard

By Kate Kenny
The Conversation, December 13, 2014

Think whistleblowing is a matter of telling the truth? Think again. "Successful" whistleblowing, in which the protagonist actually manages to make themselves [him- or herself] heard in the media and get the support of the public, is a matter of luck.

Last month a new whistleblower emerged to tell us about the goings-on in a well-known bank, JPMorgan. Alayne Fleischmann gave her description of how the firm handled the approaching car crash in the market for packaging and reselling mortgage debt. She joins the small but important number of fellow banking whistle-blowers. From Ireland's Jonathan Sugarman and Olivia Greene to the U.K.'s Paul Moore, some people did try to speak up about the misdeeds that lead to the global financial crash.

Fleischmann is a little different however—she is working on a deadline. Time is running out to prosecute her former employers. Fleischmann would like to see convictions on the basis of wire fraud, which in the U.S. has a 10-year statute of limitation—and it's already been eight since she witnessed the alleged events she has described. The clock is ticking and Fleischmann is making an appeal for people to listen to her story.

This well-spoken securities lawyer is bravely forgoing any future career in banking by forcing herself into the limelight to make this point. Statistically, a whistle-blower is unlikely to work in their industry again. As she told *Rolling Stone* journalist Matt Taibbi, "The assumption they make is that I won't blow up my life to do it . . . But they're wrong about that."

So what's luck got to do with it? Well, if Fleischmann had read the research on whistleblowing she would know that most whistleblowers' stories are simply not heard. In the vast majority of cases, people who speak out suffer in silence, alone and unheard. There is a way of drawing the attention of the public and the media. But it is an elusive one.

Successful whistleblowers are not those with the most shocking truths, but rather they are the ones who happen to tap into a current trend. Their stories match up with what the media are excited about, what the public are angry about, or what the politicians can use for political capital at that particular time. Rather depressingly, therefore, the truth is a matter of trends.

Need convincing? Look at Rudolf Elmer, the Swiss banker who tried for years to alert the media in his own nation about his bank's alleged role in the process of tax evasion. He became involved in a protracted dispute with his bank, which made allegations of forgery and theft against him.

He was painted as a thief and a blackmailer by journalists in Switzerland and even imprisoned for over six months. Fearful for his future and his family, Elmer agonized about what to do, until something dawned on him: the realpolitik of whistleblowing. Switzerland didn't want to hear, but perhaps another country would.

Elmer contacted *The Guardian* and was welcomed warmly. The U.K., and most of Europe, was trying to clamp down on the assistance Swiss banks might offer to wealthy citizens who want to avoid tax. There was an appetite for his story, and through the newspaper, and Wikileaks, he made his story public. Elmer, in other words, tapped into a trend in the U.K. when there was no such appetite in Switzerland.

Many other banking whistleblowers have found that trends are important. When I was interviewing banking whistleblowers for my book on this topic, it came up again and again. For example, Paul Moore at HBOS managed to appear on the BBC to tell his story about the overheated sales culture at the Halifax. It was just at the time of the U.K. Treasury Select Committee, when the public was screaming for news of why the banks had collapsed. Politicians were delighted to see him coming—and he was celebrated in the media.

While Moore suffered for his disclosures, fortuitous timing meant he could tell his story and counter any of the usual smearing by his former employer or backlash by the media. Likewise, Eileen Foster, a whistleblower at Countrywide (later Bank of America) in the U.S. was contacted by the influential TV show *60 Minutes*—and this was very helpful for her campaign for justice.

Now, back to Wall Street and Fleischmann's struggle to draw attention to events at her former bank. She should try to figure out how she can tap into current political and media trends. It sounds shallow, and somewhat cynical, but when it comes to other whistleblowers, it does appear that "truth" is contingent—it depends on the time and the place. Insert yourself into the news cycle and you might just avoid being crushed by the wheels.

What does this say about the value society places on whistleblowing? If the truth is not enough to get attention, perhaps there is a problem with the way whistleblowers are perceived. Even the most honest whistle-blowers have been seen as suspicious figures, a cultural perception that persists in our media and our institutions.

Groups that support and help whistleblowers have been trying hard to change this perception, and a great example is G.A.P.'s Whistleblower Tour, which brings people's real-life experiences to audiences across the United States. Transparency International Ireland has hosted similar events. Culture change is not easy, but these groups are trying.

Whistleblowing remains something of a lottery. Is this a fair way to treat whistleblowers, to leave their lives up to chance? Until there is a more robust system for listening to genuine public interest disclosures, it looks like this is all we've got.

Whistleblowers Score a Big Payday: Three Individuals, One Firm to Receive $170 Million in Bank of America Probe

By Christina Rexrode and Timothy W. Martin
The Wall Street Journal, December 19, 2014

There is a new winner in the biggest bank settlement to come out of the financial crisis: whistleblowers.

Four whistleblowers will collect a total of more than $170 million for helping investigators get a record $16.65 billion penalty against Bank of America Corp., among the biggest such payouts to tipsters in history.

The payments, to three individuals and a small New Jersey mortgage company, are in exchange for the whistleblowers' cooperation in a probe into Bank of America's mortgage practices in the years leading up to the financial crisis.

The whistleblower lawsuits accuse the bank or the firm it acquired in 2008, Countrywide Financial Corp., of misdeeds like inflating the value of mortgage properties and selling defective loans to investors. The payments, which were sent out this week, also underscore how the bank's purchase of Countrywide continues to haunt the Charlotte, N.C., firm.

The allegations trace a familiar pattern, but the whistleblower rewards provide a new wrinkle.

The size of the payments is "unprecedented in the financial sector," said Richard Moberly, a law professor at the University of Nebraska–Lincoln who researches whistleblower cases. The biggest whistleblower awards have typically been associated with drug companies or health-care frauds, he said.

The rewards, some of which were disclosed this week in court filings, are the result of separate lawsuits the whistleblowers filed against Bank of America and were then folded into the bank's global settlement in August.

"These matters have been fully resolved," a bank spokesman said Friday, referring to the whistleblowers' allegations.

The three individuals will each receive payments of tens of millions of dollars, and the mortgage company, Mortgage Now of Shrewsbury, N.J., will receive about $8.5 million, according to court filings and people familiar with the rewards.

Prosecutors and regulators are increasingly making big payouts to tipsters who help them ferret out financial misconduct. The Securities and Exchange

Commission in September announced that an informer would collect a record whistleblower award of more than $30 million, more than twice as much as the highest previous award.

Attorney General Eric Holder also said this year that he wants to boost payouts to motivate insiders to come forward with useful information.

Robert Madsen, a former employee of LandSafe Appraisal, a property appraisal company owned by Bank of America, will collect roughly $56 million, according to a person close to the situation. He had filed a complaint against the bank in 2011. Bank of America acquired LandSafe when it bought Countrywide. LandSafe is among the mortgage affiliates that Bank of America is trying to sell.

Mr. Madsen started working there around 2007. According to Mr. Madsen, his bosses started cutting his hours after he raised concerns about properties potentially being overvalued at the expense of borrowers and investors.

Mr. Madsen said he initially thought his case was a long shot, but pursued the lawsuit to protect his family. Along the way, he came to view the case as a way to stoke awareness about the importance of reliable appraisals. When "we don't know what the houses are worth, that undermines virtually every bond, every tranche, every investment instrument out there," Mr. Madsen said.

Mr. Madsen, who lives in Northern California, left the bank around early 2013 and started a company to help banks, investors and other clients identify potential fraud in appraisal work.

Shareef Abdou, a former Countrywide manager, will receive about $48 million for his cooperation in the investigation, a person familiar with the matter said. Mr. Abdou is on a leave of absence from Bank of America.

Mr. Abdou's complaint alleged that the bank sold defective mortgage loans to mortgage-finance companies Fannie Mae and Freddie Mac.

"He was able to indicate that there was an institutional breakdown within the bank, and this was a systemic problem, not an isolated incident," said Brian Mahany, a Milwaukee-based attorney who represents Mr. Abdou.

Edward O'Donnell, a former Countrywide executive, will collect nearly $58 million, according to a court filing this week. Mr. O'Donnell had originally filed suit against the bank in 2012, with allegations that are similar to Mr. Abdou's. His lawsuit created the basis for the government's successful case against the bank over a Countrywide mortgage program called the "Hustle," which U.S. authorities said churned out large numbers of mortgage loans without regard for quality.

Bank of America plans to appeal the Hustle verdict, and Mr. O'Donnell hasn't received a financial award from the government for that suit, according to his lawyer. The payout for Mr. O'Donnell will come thanks to a separate, similar lawsuit he filed in June against Countrywide and Bank of America.

Bank of America bought Countrywide in 2008. It said that the Hustle program ended before it bought Countrywide.

The company that filed a whistleblower suit, Mortgage Now, had accused Bank of America in 2012 of misrepresenting loans that it submitted to the Federal

Housing Administration for reimbursement, according to one of the lawyers who worked on the case, Clifford Marshall.

A combined $1 billion of the $16.65 billion settlement was allotted to the three cases filed by the individual whistleblowers. Their payouts will all amount to roughly 16%.

Mr. Mahany declined to say what Mr. Abdou plans to do with the money. "He's a very private individual. I don't think he likes the notoriety of the case," said Mr. Mahany. "He would just as soon go on with his life."

Too Big to Jail?

By Michael G. Winston
Government Accountability Project, October 13, 2013

In late December 2012, Swiss bank UBS agreed to pay $1.5 billion in fines to international regulators following a probe into the rigging of a key global interest rate. In admitting to fraud, Switzerland's largest bank became the second bank, after Barclays, to settle over the rate-rigging scandal. The fine, to be paid to authorities in the U.S., Britain and Switzerland, came just over a week after HSBC agreed to pay nearly $2 billion for alleged money laundering, transferring funds through the U.S. from Mexican drug cartels and nations under international sanctions like Iran.

Just weeks later, Bank of America agreed to pay mortgage finance firm Fannie Mae $10.35 billion to settle agency mortgage repurchase claims on loans it originated and sold to Fannie Mae through year-end 2008.

Months later, the U.S. Department of Justice filed its first lawsuit against a company over mortgage loans sold to big mortgage financiers, which were bailed out in 2008. The defendant is Bank of America, the owner of now-disgraced Countrywide Financial Corporation, once the largest mortgage lender in the country.

The suit was filed for fraud over "toxic" mortgage loans sold by Countrywide. Because of this, millions of Americans are paying more on their mortgages than their homes are worth. Millions more face foreclosure. Millions of jobs have vanished.

For a nation hungry for genuine accountability for the events that led to our economy's implosion, this announcement suggests that, perhaps, justice is near. But I'm not holding my breath. The unwillingness to hold people accountable for such wrongdoing is a very real problem with our current strategy in addressing malfeasance in the financial sector, and calls for a viable solution. This not only affects people in every state, it is also a global issue of potentially apocalyptic proportions.

"The fraudulent conduct alleged in the complaint was spectacularly brazen in scope," said the U.S. attorney filing the suit, which seeks at least $1 billion in penalties.

"Brazen" is the right word. I have seen this conduct up close.

Journalists covering my story have called me the "whistleblower who conquered Countrywide." At this point, though, my experience is more like whistling in the wind.

In 2009, after serving several years as Managing Director, Enterprise Chief Leadership Officer for Countrywide and Bank of America, I filed a lawsuit against them for their often abusive practices. After months of their evasive tactics and a nearly month-long jury trial, we had a verdict. On February 3, 2011, the jury vindicated me and held Countrywide/BOA accountable for wrongdoing in violation of public policy.

As an ex-employee, I am (I believe) the only individual who has compelled testimony in court of Countrywide's top officers—including cofounder, CEO and chairman of the board Angelo Mozilo—and convince a jury of their wrongdoing.

The jury found Bank of America/Countrywide guilty and awarded me damages. I am still waiting for justice. They have paid nothing, brazenly acting as if they are above the law. They stall, evade and stonewall. Later, after "shopping for justice," they had the jury verdict and court ruling reversed.

Why, *five years* after the fraud and irresponsible actions of companies like Countrywide brought us to the brink of total collapse, have there been no prosecutions against key executives? Is our justice system incapable of pressing these cases to their rightful conclusion? Or just unwilling?

In 2009 the Securities and Exchange Commission brought a civil suit against Mozilo and his colleagues for fraud and insider trading. The case never saw the inside of a courtroom. It was quietly settled, and Mozilo paid only about one-third of his penalty. Who paid the other two-thirds? Taxpayers.

These banks were accused of fraud and contributing to financial decline not seen since the Great Depression. Is it no longer a crime to defraud customers and shareholders? Enormous sums of money are set aside as "reserves" to cover litigation and settlements. Financial pay-offs are thought to be "the cost of doing business."

In the 1980s savings and loans debacle, prosecutors sent more than 800 bank officials to jail. Enron, WorldCom and Arthur Andersen all brought criminal prosecutions and jail time for people at the top.

Total number of bank officers responsible for the 2008 meltdown who have gone to jail? Zero. Where are the Charles Keatings, the Michael Milkens and the Kenneth Lays of the 2008–09 disaster?

Punishment is not the only way to modify behavior, but it works. Instead, executives now realize that they face virtually no consequences for reckless lending, exotic investments and fraud. Thus, these actions continue.

Haven't we had enough evasion? I don't believe the American people want to settle. We want to see the malfeasant held accountable and punished.

Isn't it time law-enforcement officials satisfied their commitment to transparency, responsibility and accountability?

Hedge Fund Kept U.S. Inquiry Quiet

By Gretchen Morgenson
The New York Times, December 6, 2014

In the volatile world of high finance, hedge funds come and hedge funds go. So there was little fanfare last week, apart from a few upset investors, when Vertical Capital, with $1.4 billion under management, suddenly announced it was unwinding its $400 million hedge fund operation.

Behind the scenes, however, is a troubling Wall Street story, redeemed, in part, by a whistleblower who was not willing to go along with what she viewed as dubious business practices.

In a letter to investors sent during the evening of Dec. 2, Vertical said it was negotiating with the Securities and Exchange Commission to settle a civil securities fraud case against its founder, Brett Graham, and its related brokerage firm, VCAP Securities. The commission concluded that VCAP, overseen by Mr. Graham, violated securities laws when it liquidated five collateralized debt obligations in 2012, the letter said. The broker made improper bids during the liquidations because it was "in the possession of confidential information" that gave it "an unfair advantage over other bidders," the letter said.

The letter said it expected the S.E.C. settlement to require VCAP to close and Mr. Graham to pay a fine and be barred from the industry for a period of time. The S.E.C. cited no violations by Vertical Capital.

Jonathan Gasthalter, a spokesman for Vertical, declined to elaborate on the S.E.C. investigation and did not make any of the firm's executives available for comment. Vertical, based in Midtown Manhattan, was founded in 2002 by Mr. Graham, a longtime Bear Stearns executive. Until 2006, Bank of America was a minority investor in Vertical.

In addition to its hedge fund, Vertical is a manager of collateralized debt obligations that contain bundles of mortgage loans. As a manager, Vertical decides which loans are bundled into the securities.

Not surprisingly, some of Vertical's C.D.O.s didn't do so well in the mortgage mess. One was featured in the fraud case filed last year by the Justice Department against Standard & Poor's, the credit rating agency. Vertical was the collateral manager overseeing a $1.5 billion deal in early 2007, the lawsuit said. Citibank invested $15 million in a piece of the security that was rated AAA by S.&P.; six months later,

---

the C.D.O. collapsed and Citibank lost its entire investment, the Justice Department said.

Vertical is registered with the S.E.C. as an investment adviser and counts mostly institutional investors as clients, regulatory filings show. According to a recent Vertical pitch book, its hedge fund operation has performed well. The composite net return for various funds was 377 percent for the period beginning in October 2009 and ending in August. (Vertical prepared the returns, a footnote stated, and they were not independently verified.)

But the hedge fund world is a crowded place, and hoping to drum up new investors, Vertical hired Miriam Freier as director of marketing and investor relations in June 2013. In an interview last week, Ms. Freier said she traveled extensively introducing investors to Vertical's funds; within a year, she had brought in $50 million. Another investor was preparing to invest $25 million.

But in September, Ms. Freier said, she received disturbing information from a prospective Vertical investor. As part of his due diligence, the investor filed a Freedom of Information Act request with the S.E.C. about the firm. The commission responded with a letter declining to provide the requested information because Vertical was under investigation.

This was news to Ms. Freier, whose job it was to keep Vertical's clients up on firm developments.

"I emailed the partners of the firm and said, 'What is going on?'" she said in the interview. "They started slowly disclosing things to me but not to any other employees."

She offered to speak with the S.E.C. and with investors to fulfill what she believed were the firm's disclosure duties. But her superiors warned her not to tell anyone about the investigation until the firm's negotiations with the S.E.C. were completed.

Weeks passed. Ms. Freier said she felt angry about having to live a lie in her job. By November, she was out of patience. "I didn't want to be there anymore," she said.

The company asked her to stay on until mid-February to help advise investors about the hedge fund's wind-down. Around Thanksgiving, Vertical offered her a separation agreement outlining pay terms and obligations.

The terms were unacceptable to both Ms. Freier and to Jonathan Sack, her employment lawyer at Sack & Sack. He asked the firm for additional pay for Ms. Freier and indemnification against any fines or judgments that might be awarded against her related to the regulatory problems.

Vertical refused and fired Ms. Freier on December 3. She had already begun calling investors to tell them what she had experienced at the firm. Ms. Freier is also offering to give information about the firm to the S.E.C. as a whistleblower.

Vertical is now treating Ms. Freier as a traitor. Of her requests for additional pay and indemnification, Mr. Gasthalter said: "After reaching a mutual agreement on an amicable separation, this disgruntled, now former employee sought to extort the company."

Lewis D. Lowenfels, a securities law expert in New York, said the situation at Vertical highlighted the importance of prompt disclosures by money managers today.

"At a time when whistle-blowing is widespread and encouraged by the S.E.C., investment advisers must be particularly careful to make timely and accurate disclosures of information that would be material to investors," he said.

On the matter of timing, Mr. Gasthalter said, "Vertical Capital informed investors the day after receiving the initial draft of a proposed settlement from the S.E.C."

Late last week, Mr. Sack sued Vertical on Ms. Freier's behalf. "Thankfully, the whistle-blower protections of Dodd-Frank offer a remedy for victims of retaliation," he said. "While I'm always surprised to see the ruthlessness of people in the workplace, in this instance, the acts of desperation and greed at the expense of my client's career and reputation reach new lows."

For her part, Ms. Freier said she was still absorbing what went on at Vertical. "Investors have a right to know when a firm is under an S.E.C. investigation that could result in the wind-down of a fund," she said. "They also have the right to know if a key person making investment decisions on their portfolios could be at risk of being removed from the industry as a result of a settlement with the S.E.C."

She added: "Investors are putting their trust in money managers not only to oversee their assets but also to communicate and be transparent about any issue which could potentially impact their investment."

Vertical's hedge fund investors, waiting to get their capital back, might agree.

The Man Who Blew the Whistle

By Joe Nocera
The New York Times, August 18, 2014

Late last month, the Securities and Exchange Commission issued an oblique press release announcing that it was awarding an unnamed whistleblower $400,000 for helping expose a financial fraud at an unnamed company. The money was the latest whistleblower award—there have been 13 so far—paid as part of the Dodd-Frank financial reform law, which includes both protections for whistleblowers and financial awards when their information leads to fines of more than $1 million.

The law also prevents the S.E.C. from doing anything to publicly identify the whistleblowers—hence, the circumspect press release. But through a mutual friend, I discovered the identity of this particular whistleblower, who, it turned out, was willing to tell his story.

His name is Bill Lloyd. He is 56 years old, and he spent 22 years as an agent for MassMutual Financial Group, the insurance company based in Springfield, Mass. Although companies often label whistle-blowers as disgruntled employees, Lloyd didn't fit that category. On the contrary, he liked working for MassMutual, and he was a high performer. He also is a straight arrow—"a square," said the mutual friend who introduced us—who cares about his customers; when faced with a situation where his customers were likely to get ripped off, he couldn't look the other way.

In September 2007, at a time when money was gushing into variable annuities, MassMutual added two income guarantees to make a few of its annuity products especially attractive to investors. Called Guaranteed Income Benefit Plus 6 and Guaranteed Income Benefit Plus 5, they guaranteed that the annuity income stream would grow to a predetermined cap regardless of how the investment itself performed.

Then, upon retirement, the investors had the right to take 6 percent (or 5 percent, depending on the product) of the cap for as long as they wanted or until it ran out of money, and still be able, at some point, to annuitize it. It is complicated, but the point is that thanks to the guarantee, the money was never supposed to run out. That is what the prospectus said, and it is what those in the sales force, made up of people like Lloyd, were taught to sell to customers. It wasn't long before investors had put $2.5 billion into the products.

The following July, Lloyd—and a handful of others in the sales force—discovered, to their horror, that the guarantee didn't work as advertised. In fact, because of the market's fall, it was a near-certainty that thousands of customers were going to run through the income stream within seven or eight years of withdrawing money.

Lloyd did not immediately run to the S.E.C. Rather, he dug in at MassMutual and, as the S.E.C. press release put it, did "everything feasible to correct the issue internally." For a while, he thought he was going to have success, but, at a certain point, someone stole the files he had put together on the matter and turned them over to the Financial Industry Regulatory Authority, which is the industry's self-regulatory body. It was only when the regulatory authority failed to act that his lawyer told him about the whistle-blower provisions in Dodd-Frank and he went to the S.E.C., which began its own investigation.

The Dodd-Frank law has provisions intended to protect whistle-blowers from retaliation, but there are certain aspects of being a whistleblower that it can't do anything about. "People started treating me like a leper," recalls Lloyd. "They would see me coming and turn around and walk in the other direction." Convinced that the company was laying the groundwork to fire him, he quit in April 2011, a move that cost him both clients and money. (Lloyd has since found employment with another financial institution. For its part, MassMutual says only that "we are pleased to have resolved this matter with the S.E.C.")

In November 2012, MassMutual agreed to pay a $1.6 million fine; Lloyd's $400,000 award is 25 percent of that. It was a slap on the wrist, but more important, the company agreed to lift the cap. This will cost MassMutual a lot more, but it will protect the investors who put their money—and their retirement hopes—on Mass-Mutual's guarantees. Thanks to Lloyd, the company has fixed the defect without a single investor losing a penny.

Ever since the passage of Dodd-Frank reform, the financial industry has been none too happy about the whistle-blower provisions, and there have been rumblings that congressional Republicans might try to roll back some of it. The S.E.C. now has an Office of the Whistleblower, and a website where potential whistleblowers can report fraud. It has given out $16 million in whistle-blower awards.

There are, without question, parts of the Dodd-Frank law that are problematic, not least the provisions dealing with the Too Big to Fail institutions.

But the whistleblower provisions? They are working as intended. That is the moral of Bill Lloyd's story.

A Whistleblower Spurs
Self-Scrutiny in College Sports

By Brad Wolverton
The Chronicle of Higher Education, September 12, 2014

Since exposing academic fraud at the University of North Carolina at Chapel Hill, Mary C. Willingham says she has heard from dozens of tutors and academic advisers describing similar problems on other campuses.

But few of those people have championed her cause, reflecting what some observers see as a culture of fearfulness and defensiveness in big-time athletics.

"It's really hard to embrace someone when you're holding your own breath," says Brian Davis, a former head of academic services for football at the University of Texas at Austin. "It's like, 'Please, God, don't let this happen to us.'"

Before she became the focus at Chapel Hill, Ms. Willingham was not well known in the academic-support world. But her crusade—though mired in controversy—has highlighted widespread problems, including a growing academic gap between high-profile athletes and other students, and increasingly sophisticated schemes to maintain player eligibility.

At North Carolina, Ms. Willingham says she worked with some 50 football and basketball players a year who read below a middle-school level. She provided details about hundreds of athletes enrolled in independent-study courses that required little to no work.

Ms. Willingham's critics have sought to discredit her, arguing that she misinterpreted data about athletes' reading levels, plagiarized in parts of her own master's thesis, and embellished the role of the athletic department in steering players toward the bogus classes.

The whistleblower and her critics appear to be operating on different levels. North Carolina's administrators seem to think that, by undermining the messenger, they can defend the integrity of the flagship campus. But Ms. Willingham has a bigger target. She sees the university's problems as a microcosm of a broken educational enterprise that she is intent on fixing.

"We start in kindergarten and we don't stop," she said in a recent interview. "We take money and resources away from poor black families. Then we bring these kids to college, and they make money for us without getting a real education."

Elephant in the Room

Soon after Ms. Willingham's accusations went public, through a series of articles in *The News & Observer,* a North Carolina newspaper, many academic advisers posted comments on a popular industry forum, raising questions about how the scandal would be perceived nationally and what other athletic departments could do to prevent similar fallout.

Early this year, several directors of academic support for athletes commented on the increasing prevalence of underprepared athletes and the complicity of academic-support systems. Until Ms. Willingham started talking about such issues, some directors said in the online forum, few people were willing to discuss them publicly.

"College athletics has become a monster of an elephant in the room that has aspects (e.g., academic unpreparedness) which folks—coaches, provosts, admissions, presidents, alumni, even us in academic services—convince themselves don't exist," wrote one director, in a post that was shared with *The Chronicle.* "Who among us, in our tenure in this profession, hasn't raised an eyebrow how a certain student-athlete got admitted to our institution? Who among us has never had an instance where a coach has 'impressed' upon us the need for Johnny or Susie to 'be eligible?'

"Unless the NCAA is going to seriously ramp up requirements, the elephant will remain in the room, largely invisible," said the director, who requested anonymity because of the potential for professional reprisal.

While some advisers posted concerns about Ms. Willingham's methods, her campaign has helped persuade many athletic departments to scrutinize their protections against academic fraud.

Prompted in part by the widening scandal in Chapel Hill, leaders of the National Association of Academic Advisors for Athletics recently unveiled new guidelines for promoting academic integrity. Their suggestions include dozens of ideas for tightening oversight of nontraditional classes, tutoring sessions, and computer labs.

The document, which the group's leaders shared with *The Chronicle,* raises concerns about the proctoring of online exams and assignments, coaches' involvement in nontraditional courses, and the need for policies that specify how suspicious activity should be reported.

The guidelines also suggest that colleges should create policies specifying appropriate communication among faculty members, coaches, and athletics administrators.

In response to the scandal, administrators at Chapel Hill have adopted a number of safeguards, including requiring professors to submit to regular class checks to ensure that courses are meeting as scheduled. The university has also created learning contracts for independent-study classes and has restructured its academic-support unit.

The UNC scandal has had an impact elsewhere as well. The University of Texas has encouraged its academic advisers to examine the relationships that some professors have with players, says Mr. Davis, who worked at the university for about 16 years before departing last month.

"It made us look at making sure that student-athletes don't have the opportunity to take advantage of some faculty member's kindness," he says. "I don't know if the industry is there yet, but you can't just assume that if a faculty member wants to do something, it's the right thing to do. You have to be the one that controls the moral compass."

Other universities have devoted more time to training, emphasizing how much help tutors are allowed to give players.

"Half the time, when you have a tutor who does too much, it's not because anyone has asked them to do it, it's because they're nice people," says one academic-support leader, who asks not to be identified. "They'll say, 'He's really going to struggle with this, so I'm going to help him more.'

"You can convince yourself it's OK," this person says. "But you really have to check yourself in those situations."

Limited Safeguards

Monitoring online classes, which have become increasingly popular with athletes, remains a significant challenge. Many programs have struggled to define how much assistance their academic-support staff can provide for distance learning. And with the rapid growth of such offerings, some institutions have failed to put in place safeguards verifying the identity of the person taking the class.

Athletes who take online classes sometimes have their tests proctored in athletic-department computer labs where others are studying, raising concerns that players might be receiving inappropriate assistance.

In recent months, academic advisers have debated whether test-taking should be allowed in such spaces, and if so, how it should be monitored.

Ursula Gurney, a senior athletic director at the University of Missouri at Kansas City, says the subject came up in April at a regional meeting of academic advisers in Oklahoma City. During a discussion in which she was a panelist, someone suggested that athletes who are taking tests in computer labs should be properly identified.

Ms. Gurney s university will soon require that a red sign be placed over the computer space of test-takers, signaling to others that they need to be working independently.

"We all need to make sure we're improving our systems to create a more sound environment," she says.

The problems at Chapel Hill have reaffirmed her belief that, to prevent fraud, athletic departments must foster more communication between athletics officials and academic officials.

"Whoever is leading the academic effort needs to be engaged with senior administrators so they're well-versed in what's going on—how tutoring takes place, the admissions process, who's eligible," Ms. Gurney says. "Academics cannot be a silo within the athletic department—it needs to be part of the team, just like strength and conditioning or the training room."

North Carolina's troubles have led many people to question how deeply academic-support units should be embedded in athletic departments.

In the late 1990s, after an academic scandal on the men's basketball team at the University of Minnesota–Twin Cities, many athletics programs shifted oversight of academic advising to the provost or chief academic officer. For various reasons, including financial challenges at many institutions, the pendulum has started to swing the other way, or has landed somewhere in the middle.

Many advising units now have dual reporting lines, says Kim Durand, associate athletics director for student development at the University of Washington, who is president of the national academic advisers' group.

"A lot of people get their funding from athletics but have oversight and a connection with campus," she says. "But is it seen as a no-no or not as favorable or that there's more potential for fraud when you only report to athletics? I haven't seen that."

Critics disagree, saying that, as long as academic advisers continue to take their orders from athletics officials, their ability to speak out about problems will be compromised.

"They have no business answering to an athletic entity—they need to be housed in the academic organization under the provost," says Gerald Gurney, a former director of academic services for athletes at the University of Oklahoma. "It's the only thing that will set academic-support professionals free from undue pressure."

And as important as advisers are in helping to maintain academic integrity, they face other limits. For example, they typically have no say in who is admitted to the university.

If colleges hope to more fully insulate themselves from academic fraud, critics argue, they must adopt tougher admissions standards rather than accept anyone who meets the NCAA's minimum qualifications.

"College presidents know full well they are admitting unprepared athletes on the pretense of being students," Mr. Gurney says. "Until they do something to change that, academic fraud is only going to get worse."

"In It To Win It"

Ms. Willingham, a former learning specialist, figures that colleges will always accept athletes who are not at the same academic level as their peers, and she has no problem with that. She just wants institutions to do more to support those players so they have a better chance to succeed.

She would like to see the NCAA pay for an extensive remedial-education program for the lowest academic performers, requiring those athletes to sit out games and have limited practice time for the first 15 months they are on campus.

"For me, it all goes back to literacy," she says. "If you're not ready to read a college text, then you need to get prepared before you can really pass a class."

This week Ms. Willingham plans to visit Washington for a meeting of the Knight Commission on Intercollegiate Athletics. It will be her eighth visit to Washington in the past nine months.

During that time, she has met with aides to a half-dozen members of Congress who have taken an increasing interest in overhauling the NCAA. She says she has also adopted a slogan: "I'm 'in it to win it'—as the NCAA says."

For her, a victory on the national level would mean that the graduation rates of black men continue to rise, and that more of them begin to read closer to grade level.

She also wants an open, honest conversation about the eligibility of athletes.

"What's more important?" she asks. "The eligibility, or education and future of these young people?"

New Efforts to Thwart Academic Fraud

In the wake of a scandal at the University of North Carolina, the Chapel Hill campus was one of several that made changes to guard against academic fraud in athletics programs. Here are some highlights:

U. of Alabama at Tuscaloosa

* Increased training for tutors, requiring an additional session with compliance officers every semester.
* Began conducting exit interviews with 10 to 12 tutors to assess potential gaps in training or other problems.

U. of North Carolina at Chapel Hill
* Required professors to submit to regular class checks to ensure the validity of courses.
* Created learning contracts for independent-study classes.
* Restructured its academic-support unit for athletes.

U. of Texas at Austin
* Adopted stricter regulations for tutors, including requirements for athletes to work with different tutors on different papers.
* More closely examined the relationships that some professors have with players.

U. of Washington
* Established explicit contracts for students who enroll in independent studies and began requiring department chairs to approve such classes.
* Analyzed its expectations for independent studies, to ensure that the credit hours awarded reflect the work being done.

By talking publicly about problems at the U. of North Carolina at Chapel Hill, Mary Willingham has revealed the "elephant in the room," one insider says.

Whistleblowers Need Encouragement, Not Roadblocks

By Curtis C. Verschoor
Strategic Finance, October 2013

It's well understood that a whistleblower is the most important source of evidence in detecting fraud and other misdeeds and convicting the criminal or enforcing a civil statute. The whistleblower program at the U.S. Securities & Exchange Commission (SEC) has allowed many individuals to report securities laws violations. But companies and their counsel are reportedly impeding would-be whistleblowers in violation of the law. In addition, the Internal Revenue Service (IRS) and U.S. Commodity Futures Trading Commission (CFTC) whistleblower initiatives appear to require streamlining to improve their effectiveness.

The Dodd-Frank Act enables the SEC to pay cash to whistleblowers who report significant wrongdoing (more than $1 million in sanctions). In November 2012, then SEC Chairman Mary L. Schapiro reported, "In just its first year, the whistleblower program already has proven to be a valuable tool in helping us ferret out financial fraud. When insiders provide us with high-quality road maps of fraudulent wrongdoing, it reduces the length of time we spend investigating and saves the agency substantial resources."

The second cash award under the SEC's whistleblower program was announced June 12, 2013. The SEC will award three whistleblowers 15% of the total amount recovered by the government in return for tips and information they provided to help the SEC and the Justice Department stop a sham hedge fund. The total reward is expected to amount to approximately $125,000. Whistleblowers are paid from the SEC's Investor Protection Fund, which held more than $453 million at the end of the 2012 fiscal year.

Additional and larger awards are expected in the future. The SEC Office of the Whistleblower had posted 76 orders in 2013 (through August), each with monetary sanctions exceeding $1 million. These include well-known defendants such as U.S. technology company IBM, Dutch bank ABN AMRO, Swiss bank UBS Securities, and French oil company Total S.A. According to whistleblower attorney Jordan Thomas, "There has been a green line that financial services professionals have historically feared to cross, but they are now more willing to break their silence because of the SEC Whistleblower Program." He added, "In the coming years, I predict many of the SEC's most significant cases will be the result of whistleblowers who report their tips to the agency."

Obstacles

A court decision in Houston, Texas, involving General Electric (GE) may confound the protective rights of whistleblowers to be shielded from retaliatory acts of their employer. The plaintiff was a former executive at GE who alleged he was fired because he was a whistleblower. GE, however, claimed that the executive never reported it to the SEC, blurring the SEC's definition of a "whistleblower." The court stated that "without any allegation that he reported a securities-law violation to the SEC, [the plaintiff] is not a 'whistleblower' under Dodd-Frank." GE stated its "consistent position has been that employees should report internally first, with lawsuits and bounties reserved for instances where a company fails to respond appropriately, obliging employees to report to the SEC." The plaintiff's attorney is contemplating an appeal to the U.S. Supreme Court.

The case hinges on the issue of whether the Dodd-Frank Act protects whistleblowers in general or just those who report misdeeds to the SEC. Several courts held earlier that all whistleblowers were covered under Dodd-Frank and thus were protected from reprisal. It appears that whistleblowers need legal representation to help determine the appropriate strategy, as recommended by the *IMA® Statement of Ethical Professional Practice*.

Another potential obstacle to the effectiveness of the SEC's whistleblowing initiative was pointed out in a May 8, 2013, letter to the SEC from whistleblower attorneys David J. Marshall and Debra S. Katz. They assert that

> companies routinely include in separation agreements [restrictions] that undercut Congress' purpose in creating the SEC's whistleblower-reward program:
>
> 1. The requirement that the whistleblower renounce the right to receive any award the SEC might make as the result of a successful enforcement action; and
>
> 2. Requirements that an employee disclose to the company all past or future communications with any third party, including government agencies, and/or that the employee agree to cooperate with the company in any ensuing investigation by the SEC.

According to Marshall and Katz, companies continue to devise ways to restrict whistleblowers despite SEC rules stating that "no person may take any action to impede an individual from communicating directly with the Commission staff about a possible securities law violation." They continued, "The inclusion of such terms in severance agreements and settlement agreements resolving employment claims has a chilling effect on individuals who would provide information to the SEC about potential securities violations." The SEC's discussion of its Final Rule under Dodd-Frank Section 21F states that Section 29(a) of the Exchange Act (of which the Dodd-Frank Act is a part) specifically states, "Employers may not require employees to waive or limit their anti-retaliation rights under Section 21F."

In their letter to the SEC, Marshall and Katz noted that employees may not have legal counsel or much time to decide whether to sign a severance agreement favorable to their employer. In their view, such pressure undermines the protections from retaliatory acts that Congress and the SEC intended to afford whistleblowers. They recommend the SEC issue clarifying regulations "to stem the growth of an apparent effort to discourage whistleblowers from providing information to the Commission," which is the clear objective of the SEC's whistleblower reward program.

More Encouragement Needed

The whistleblower program at the IRS revealed significant activity in its 2012 fiscal year annual report. There were 332 submissions, involving 671 taxpayers, that appeared to meet the statutory threshold of $2 million of tax, penalties, and interest in dispute. Awards of more than $125 million were paid during the year to 128 whistleblowers. In fiscal year 2013, the only publicly announced award under the revised 2006 statute was a payment of $104 million made to a former banker at Swiss UBS AG—the largest payment ever. The informant provided information that resulted in UBS turning over the names of thousands of Americans suspected of being tax cheats.

The IRS annual report raised concerns that it says need to be addressed to improve the whistleblower program:

1. Protection of whistleblowers against retaliation. There are no provisions similar to those in the Dodd-Frank Act.

2. Means of providing adequate protection of confidential information of taxpayers whose taxes are at issue.

3. Clarification of the definition of "amount in dispute" and how to determine the amount of "gross income." Also, an observer may wonder why the threshold of IRS interest is $2 million rather than the $1 million in the Dodd-Frank Act.

In addition, on August 29, 2013, U.S. Attorney General Eric Holder announced a new program to encourage Swiss banks to cooperate with ongoing investigations of the use of foreign bank accounts to commit tax evasion. The Swiss government announced it would encourage Swiss banks to cooperate. "This program will significantly enhance the Justice Department's ongoing efforts to aggressively pursue those who attempt to evade the law by hiding their assets outside of the United States," Holder said.

The CFTC also has a whistleblower program initiated by Dodd-Frank, but no awards have been paid yet. During fiscal year 2012, the whistleblower office received 58 complaints and an additional 52 tips that weren't whistleblowers. The whistleblower office has created an educational program to raise awareness of its whistleblower program. Like the SEC, the CFTC has a Customer Protection Fund, which held approximately $100 million at the end of fiscal 2012.

Whistleblowing's importance to all professional accountants is further emphasized in a proposed revision to the international Code of Ethics for Professional Accountants published by the International Ethics Standards Board for Accountants (IESBA). An exposure draft titled "Responding to a Suspected Illegal Act" was released in August 2012 and has drawn 73 comment letters, including one from IMA. The objective of the new pronouncement is to "describe the circumstances in which a professional accountant is required or expected to override confidentiality and disclose the act to an appropriate authority."

As companies try to restrict whistleblowers while government agencies and organizations try to encourage and protect them, it appears increasingly important that whistleblowers follow the guidance contained in the IMA Statement of Ethical Professional Practice. It recommends that when dealing with the resolution of ethical conflict, you "consult with your own attorney as to legal obligations and rights concerning the ethical conflict."

3
Reprisals and the Law

Chelsea (formerly Bradley) Manning is escorted by military police from the courthouse at Fort Meade in Maryland.

The Backlash

In the annals of whistleblowing, there may be no stranger attempted retaliation than in the case of Daniel Ellsberg. During the Vietnam War, Ellsberg was privy to an enormous amount of damaging, confidential information about American involvement. He released his enormous cache of information to the *New York Times* in what has become known, quite famously, as the Pentagon Papers. As Andy Greenberg recounts in the book *This Machine Kills Secrets*, "Ellsberg's leak was such a blow to President Nixon's ego and sense of executive power that the White House overreacted in spectacular fashion . . . 'We've got to get him,' the president said to [Henry] Kissinger and Attorney General John Mitchell." Accordingly, the office of Ellsberg's psychotherapist suffered a White House–backed break-in, which was aimed at finding some sort of incriminating evidence amid the doctor's confidential patient files (none was found). This was followed by "an attempt to drug Ellsberg with LSD before a speech he planned to give in Washington. . . . [H]otel workers. . . were recruited by a team led by G. Gordon Liddy to infiltrate the event, spike Ellsberg's soup with acid to 'befuddle' him, and 'make him appear to be a near burnt-out drug case.'" This plan, though—for a variety of reasons—never happened.

In the 1970s, Karen Silkwood was an employee at an Oklahoma nuclear plant. She uncovered egregious safety violations and refused to be silenced. En route to meet a *New York Times* reporter and share her extensive documentation, she was killed in a mysterious car accident. Frank Serpico, who exposed an ingrained culture of corruption in the New York City police department, was almost killed in a drug-related ambush that may have been prevented—and wasn't—by other members of the force.

In retrospect, the Nixon administration's planned retaliation against Ellsberg is both twisted and funny—probably because no physical harm came to him. The cases of Silkwood and Serpico are purely and completely horrible: Karen Silkwood paid for her whistleblowing with her life and Frank Serpico came close to that grim fate. Seldom are the consequences of whistleblowing so dramatic. But it is, unfortunately, naïve to imagine that whistleblowers *won't* face concerted official pressure aimed to shut down their revelations.

True, "The government routinely offers incentives to whistleblowers—including hundreds and millions of dollars to expose tax fraud" as well as "extending protections to prevent" retaliation. (Brianna Ehley *Fiscal Times*, February 24, 2015), But there are gaping holes in these protections—including, in an incredible irony, the Department of Justice itself, "where even its own employees aren't covered by any real or effective whistleblower protections." There is simply no getting around the fact that whistleblowing is—to say the least—a gamble in which nothing is assured: not legal protection, not vindication.

"In the chain-of-command-oriented military," *Time* magazine reported, "whistle-blowers rarely fare well. Each year, hundreds of uniformed members of the military send official complaints to Inspectors General within the Department of Defense saying they are the targets of reprisal. Most do not have their claims of reprisal substantiated."

In early 2015 the Supreme Court weighed in with a ruling on the legality of whistleblowing. By a vote of 7-2, the justices ruled in favor of air marshal Robert MacLean. MacLean, according to *USA Today*, "flew undercover and armed, to thwart terrorists. When the Transportation Security Administration decided to reduce overnight flights for marshals in 2003," MacLean—fearing for the public's safety—leaked the news. The Court's decision has been interpreted as a green light for whistleblowers' continued legal protection—but only to an extent. Many of the laws and regulations protecting whistleblowers are still a patchwork of protection: The Supreme Court has not, by any means, given a comprehensive legal sanction in favor of whistleblowing. The ruling—as significant as it is—does not totally ease the plight of whistleblowers.

There are also the entrenched tactics of retaliation that can legally hide that they are, in fact, retaliation: being downsized or fired for a host of seemingly legitimate reasons; shunned by coworkers, or having one's office moved to some out-of-the-way, inhospitable locale. "The retaliation for whistleblowing can take many forms," Jillian Berman wrote in the *Huffington Post*. "In some cases, whistleblowers are left out of team meetings of discussions. . . In others, they become ineligible for a bonus or are transferred to another location." The victimized whistleblower can find him- or herself without a concrete legal case: How can you affirm, in a court of law, that you were downsized because of your whistleblowing? Or denied a bonus?

Recent years have yielded a steady stream of high-profile whistleblowers. It is impossible to avoid the case of Edward Snowden, the former government contractor "who stole a trove of highly classified documents," "now on the run from American charges of espionage and theft, and he faces the prospect of spending the rest of his life looking over his shoulder." (*New York Times* January 1, 2014) Snowden, per the *Times*, was facing the extremely serious consequences of being charged with "two violations of the Espionage Act involving unauthorized communication of classified information, and a charge of theft of government property. Those three charges carry prison sentences of 10 years each, and when the case is presented to a grand jury for indictment, the government is virtually certain to add more charges, probably adding up to a life sentence that Mr. Snowden is understandably trying to avoid." The legal protections for whistleblowers don't seem at all relevant in these high-profile cases.

Likewise, in 2013, Chelsea Manning (formerly known as Bradley Manning)—"the Army intelligence analyst who leaked the largest cache of classified documents in U.S. history" (*Washington Post* August 21, 2013)—was sentenced to 35 years in prison, convicted of "violations of the Espionage Act, for copying and disseminating classified military field reports, State Department cables, and assessments of detainees held at Guantanamo Bay, Cuba." Both Snowden and Manning—rightly or wrongly—have faced the full force of legal action and punishment against them. A salient point is that "the executive branch has enormous power over national security and the exercise of that power is not fully transparent." (Yochai Benkler *The New Republic*) Any presidential administration can easily "limit judicial oversight" in these cases. In other words, when the stakes are national security (or what is perceived to be national security), the odds are against the whistleblower.

The Espionage and Sedition Acts of 1917 "prohibited individuals from expressing or publishing opinions that would interfere with the U.S. military's effort to defeat Germany and its allies" in World War I (*Immigration in America* Web site). This gave the state enormous power to punish. The Espionage Act, nearly a century later, is still the law. It is still very much enforced: an enormous counterbalance to much of the legal protection that is afforded to whistleblowers. Nothing, legally, can mitigate perceived damage to national security, which may explain the severity of the charges against Snowden and the sentence given Manning. It is also, presumably, a caution to other potential whistleblowers. Whistleblowers "have come forward" in greater numbers, Alexandra Marks wrote for the *Christian Science Monitor.* "But new secrecy regulations and a series of judicial rulings have threatened the limited legal protections that are supposed to prevent retaliation against such whistle-blowers—even if they believe what they want to report is essential to national security."

Whistleblowers face retaliation on many different levels. There are, however, resources and assistance. The Supreme Court has put some guarantees into place. Whistleblowers can also look to Congress: According to Michael McMillan, the "Whistleblower Protection Act of 1989 was enacted to protect federal workers who report misconduct in government. . . . Section 806 of the Sarbanes-Oxley Act of 2002 provides protection for employees of public companies who provide evidence of fraud, and the 2010 Dodd-Frank Wall Street Reform and Consumer Protection Act required the SEC [Securities and Exchange Commission] to establish a whistleblower program that rewards 'individuals who offer high-quality original information. . . .'" There exists a National Whistleblowers Center (http://www.whistleblowers.org/index.php?option=com_frontpage&Itemid=71) that offers—among other things—an array of legal information.

One of the bedrocks of whistleblower-protection is the False Claims Act, which focuses on the federal government and federal contractors, according to Adam Vukovic for *LegalMatch.* The Sarbanes-Oxley Act of 2002—also known as SOX—"was implemented in response to widespread fraud being practiced by large corporations at the time. Most people associate SOX with issues such as improper corporate governance and accounting issues. However, SOX also contains a major provision which deals with whistleblowers in a corporate setting. Employees can file a claim under SOX against an employer who has violated the law. Like other federal statutes, SOX also protects such whistleblowers from employer retaliation."

There is something encouraging about these resources and the current political and judicial climate, but the downside is that these protections have been put into place because they're so necessary. "Even though more workers are witnessing violations of company rules, they're feeling pressure"—still—"not to say anything," according to Jillian Berman. "Though 65 percent of workers who saw a violation reported it—an all-time high—retaliation against whistleblowers rose to a high as well: More than a fifth of employees who reported a violation said they experienced some kind of retaliation."

Whistleblowing has theoretical legal guarantees. A legal guarantee, no matter how seemingly airtight, can wither away in the face of concerted government pressure. In the realm of state secrets, the legal guarantees are essentially nonexistent. Whistleblowing, in all its manifestations, has become a permanent part of society and government. Legal pushback—in all *its* manifestations—has also become a permanent part of whistleblowing. The only safe prediction is that these issues will continue to occupy the courts, the Congress, and the executive branch.

Bibliography

Benkler, Yochai. "The Dangerous Logic of the Bradley Manning Case." *The New Republic*, March 1, 2013; http://www.newrepublic.com/article/112554

Berman, Jillian. "Company Retaliation Against Whistleblowers Rises to All-Time High, Survey Finds." *Huffington Post*, January 6, 2012; http://www.huffington-post.com/2012/01/06/business-ethics-_n_1189110.html

Dashiell, Eddith A. "Espionage and Sedition Acts of 1917–1918." Immigration in America Web site, October 18, 2011; http://immigrationinamerica.org/482-espi-onage-and-sedition-acts-of-1917-1918.html

Devine, Tom, and Tarek F. Maassarani. *The Corporate Whistleblower's Survival Guide* (San Francisco: Berrett-Koehler, 2011).

Editorial Board. "Edward Snowden, Whistle-Blower." *New York Times*, January 1, 2014; http://www.nytimes.com/2014/01/02/opinion/edward-snowden-whistle-blower.html?_r=0

Ehley, Brianna. "GAO Outs Justice for Not Protecting Whistleblowers." *Fiscal Times*, February 24, 2015; http://www.thefiscaltimes.com/2015/02/24/GAO-Outs-Justice-Not-Protecting-Whistleblowers

Foti, Catherine. "When Is a 'Whistleblower' Not Really a 'Whistleblower'?" *Forbes*. August 7, 2013; http://www.forbes.com/sites/insider/2013/08/07/when-is-a-whistleblower-not-really-a-whistleblower/

Greenberg, Andy. *This Machine Kills Secrets: How WikiLeakers, Cypherpunks, and Hacktivists Aim to Free the World's Information* (New York: Dutton, 2012).

Higgins, Tim, and Nick Summers. "GM Recalls: How General Motors Silenced a Whistle-Blower." *Bloomberg Business*, June 18, 2014: http://www.bloomberg.com/bw/articles/2014-06-18/gm-recalls-whistle-blower-was-ignored-mary-bar-ra-faces-congress

Jansen, Bart. "Supreme Court Sides with Former TSA Air Marshal." *USA Today*, January 21, 2015: http://www.usatoday.com/story/news/2015/01/21/supreme-court-tsa-maclean-air-marshal-whistle-blower/22040645/

Marks, Alexandra. "National Security vs. Whistleblowing." *Christian Science Monitor*, January 24, 2006; http://www.csmonitor.com/2006/0124/p02s01-uspo.html

McMillan, Michael. "Retaliation Against Whistle-Blowers: No Good Deed Goes

Unpunished." *Enterprising Investor*, October 24, 2012; http://blogs.cfainstitute.
org/investor/2012/10/24/whistle-blowing-no-good-deed-goes-unpunished/

Reid, Brad. "Whistleblower Statutory Protections Are Frequently Narrowly Interpreted by Courts." *Huffington Post*, November 13, 2014; http://www.huffington-
post.com/brad-reid/whistleblower-statutory-p_b_6154148.html

Schwellenbach, Nick. "Why Military Whistleblowers Fear Reprisal." *Time*, October 20, 2011; http://nation.time.com/2011/10/20/why-military-whistleblowers-fear-
reprisal/

Tate, Julie. "Bradley Manning Sentenced to 35 Years in WikiLeaks Case." *Washington Post*, August 21, 2013; http://www.washingtonpost.com/world/national-
security/judge-to-sentence-bradley-manning-today/2013/08/20/85bee184-09d0
-11e3-b87c-476db8ac34cd_story.html

Vukovic, Adam. "Corporate Whistleblower Protection and the Sarbanes-Oxley Act." *LegalMatch*, December 12, 2014; http://www.legalmatch.com/law-library/ar-
ticle/corporate-whistleblower-protection-and-the-sarbanes-oxley-act.html

Message from the Chief of the Office of the Whistleblower

By Sean X. McKessy
Dodd-Frank Whistleblower Program, November 17, 2014

Pursuant to Section 922 of the Dodd-Frank Wall Street Reform and Consumer Protection Act ("Dodd-Frank Act"), the U.S. Securities and Exchange Commission ("Commission" or "SEC") created a whistleblower program designed to encourage the submission of high-quality information to aid Division of Enforcement ("Enforcement") staff in discovering and prosecuting violations of the federal securities laws. There are three integral components of the Commission's whistleblower program—monetary awards, retaliation protection, and confidentiality protection—each of which is equally important to the continued success of the program. During Fiscal Year 2014, the Office of the Whistleblower ("OWB" or "Office") administered the Commission's whistleblower program with an eye to furthering each of these objectives.

Fiscal Year 2014 was historic for the Office in terms of both the number and dollar amount of whistleblower awards. The Commission issued whistleblower awards to more individuals in Fiscal Year 2014 than in all previous years combined. Since the inception of the whistleblower program, the Commission has authorized awards to fourteen whistleblowers. The SEC authorized awards to nine of these whistleblowers in Fiscal Year 2014. Each of these whistleblowers provided original information that led or significantly contributed to a successful enforcement action.

Not only did the number of whistleblower awards rise significantly, but the magnitude of the award payments was record-breaking. On September 22, 2014, the Commission authorized an award of more than $30 million to a whistleblower who provided key original information that led to a successful enforcement action. The whistleblower in this matter provided information of an ongoing fraud that otherwise would have been very difficult to detect. The award is the largest made by the SEC's whistleblower program to date and the fourth award to a whistleblower living in a foreign country, demonstrating the program's international reach. We hope that awards like this one will incentivize company and industry insiders, or others who may have knowledge of possible federal securities law violations, both in the U.S. and abroad, to come forward and report their information promptly to the Commission.

Sean X. McKessy. Reprinted from the 2014 Annual Report to Congress on the Dodd-Frank Whistleblower Program, U.S. Securities and Exchange Commission

Two other whistleblower awards made this year drive home another important message—that companies not only need to have internal reporting mechanisms in place, but they must act upon credible allegations of potential wrongdoing when voiced by their employees. For example, the Commission's Final Order of July 31, 2014, reflects that the whistleblower in that matter worked aggressively internally to bring the securities law violations to the attention of appropriate company personnel. The whistleblower brought the information to the SEC only after the company failed to take corrective action. Similarly, on August 29, 2014, the Office announced a whistleblower award to a company employee with audit and compliance responsibilities who reported the securities violation internally and then reported the violation to the SEC after the company failed to take appropriate, timely action in response to the information. Persons with internal audit or compliance-related functions may be eligible under the program in certain limited circumstances, including where the individual reports the securities law violation internally and then waits 120 days before reporting the information to the Commission.

Fiscal Year 2014 also saw significant additional payments being made to individuals who had received awards in previous years. Because of the Commission's collection efforts, additional amounts were recovered in certain actions which, in turn, increased the amounts paid to whistleblowers in those matters. For example, our very first award recipient has seen the whistleblower award increase from the initial payout of nearly $50,000 to over $385,000, more than seven times the original payment amount.

Last year, OWB reported that it was coordinating actively with Enforcement staff to identify matters where retaliatory measures were taken against whistleblowers. On June 16, 2014, the Commission brought its first enforcement action under the antiretaliation provisions of the Dodd-Frank Act. In that case, the head trader of Paradigm Capital Management reported to the SEC that the company had engaged in prohibited principal transactions. After learning that the head trader reported the potential misconduct to the SEC, the firm engaged in a series of retaliatory actions, including changing the whistleblower's job function, stripping the whistleblower of supervisory responsibilities and otherwise marginalizing the whistleblower. The Commission ordered the firm to pay $2.2 million to settle the retaliation and other charges. The Commission's action sends a strong message to employers that retaliation against whistleblowers in any form is unacceptable.

The SEC also filed *amicus curiae* briefs in several private cases pending in the federal courts to address the scope of the anti-retaliation employment protections established by the Dodd-Frank Act. The Commission argued that the anti-retaliation protections should not be interpreted narrowly to reach only individuals who make disclosures directly to the Commission. Rather, the employment protections should be understood to protect individuals at publicly-traded companies from employment retaliation who internally report potential securities law violations. The SEC explained that the whistleblower program was designed to encourage employees to report internally instances of potential securities violations and was not meant to replace or undercut corporate compliance programs. But any refusal to provide anti-retaliation protection to individuals who report wrongdoing internally at public-ly-traded companies could create the unintended result of causing whistleblowers to forgo internal compliance programs and instead report directly to the SEC.

Confidentiality protection for whistleblowers also is one of the Office's paramount objectives. Confidentiality may be particularly important in cases where the whistleblower currently is employed at the company that is the subject of his or her tip or continues to work in the same or similar industry. During Fiscal Year 2014, the Office worked with other SEC staff to ensure that those who work with whistleblowers or who may review whistleblower information understand their confidentiality obligations under the Dodd-Frank Act and the Commission's implementing regulations.

As a result of the Commission's issuance of significant whistleblower awards, enforcement of the anti-retaliation provisions, and protection of whistleblower confidentiality, the agency has continued to receive an increasing number of whistleblower tips. In Fiscal Year 2014, OWB received 3,620 whistleblower tips, a more than 20% increase in the number of whistleblower tips in just two years. The Office also staffs a public hotline to answer questions from whistleblowers or their counsel concerning the whistleblower program or how to go about submitting information to the agency. In the past fiscal year, we returned over 2,731 calls from members of the public.

Finally, OWB encourages anyone who believes they have information concerning a potential securities law violation, including whether they were retaliated against for reporting the information, to submit the tip via the online portal on OWB's webpage (http://www.sec.gov/whistleblower) or by submitting a Form TCR by mail or fax, also located on OWB's webpage. If a whistleblower or his or her counsel has any question about how or whether to submit a tip to the Commission, or any other questions about the program, they should call the whistleblower hotline at (202) 551-4790.

Why Is Obama Bashing a Whistleblower Law He Already Signed?

By Dana Liebelson
Mother Jones, January 10, 2013

Remember that scene in *Mean Girls* where Regina George, the blonde queen bee, tells a classmate, "I love your skirt, where did you get it?" but then says, "That is the ugliest f-ing skirt I've ever seen," behind the other teen's back? President Barack Obama might have just pulled a similar stunt with the whistleblower community.

Obama signed a new law expanding whistleblower protections for some government employees in November, and on January 2, he signed the 2013 National Defense Authorization Act, which extends similar protections to defense contractors who expose waste and corruption. But the NDAA signing came with a caveat that blindsided the bill's backers and has some in the whistleblower community up in arms: In a signing statement, Obama wrote that the bill's whistleblowing protections "could be interpreted in a manner that would interfere with my authority to manage and direct executive branch officials," and he promised to ignore them if they conflicted with his power to "supervise, control, and correct employees' communications with the Congress in cases where such communications would be unlawful or would reveal information that is properly privileged or otherwise confidential."

"Twelve million contractors are going to be out in the cold because of this," warns Jesselyn Radack, the national security and human rights director for the Government Accountability Project and a former whistleblower. "Asking employees to go to their boss before going to Congress defeats the purpose of blowing the whistle." Radack adds that presidents "use signing statements to direct their subordinates on how to interpret and administer a law, and it can have substantial legal impact." She points to George W. Bush's signing statements on torture and the USA PATRIOT Act as examples, both of which allowed the former president to dodge parts of those laws.

"The language Obama used wasn't defined, it's completely ambiguous, and it's already led to confusion," says Angela Canterbury, director of public policy at the Project on Government Oversight. "I can imagine contractors claiming that disclosures made by whistleblowers are 'confidential,' and I think it could likely have a chilling effect."

Peter Van Buren, a former foreign service officer who wrote a book exposing contracting waste in Iraq (and was hassled by the State Department as a result) tells *Mother Jones* the signing statement "is merely another expression of [the Obama] administration's hostile policy toward all whistleblowers. . . It disappoints me, and devalues my own efforts to bring transparency to the government."

Obama didn't alert either Sen. Claire McCaskill (D-Mo.), who backed the protections, nor Rep. Jackie Speier (D-Calif.), one of the bill's sponsors, that the signing statement was coming, according to reports in the *Huffington Post* and the *Washington Post*. In a press release, Speier called Obama's signing statement "deeply disturbing," and warned it could potentially undo the language meant to protect contractor whistleblowers.

Obama has been accused of treating lawful whistleblowers like illegal leakers. His administration has wielded the World War I–era Espionage Act against more federal workers than all other presidents combined. Targets of Obama's crackdown have ranged from Thomas Drake, a former senior executive at the National Security Administration who helped expose hundreds of millions of dollars in waste on a government contract, and John Kiriakou, a former CIA agent who spoke out publicly about waterboarding and is facing prison time.

Other whistleblowers and whistleblower advocates are more optimistic—they're unhappy with the signing statement, but say they're glad they got new legal protections. "Obama's signing statement was rhetorical fluff," argues Tom Devine, the legal director of the Government Accountability Project (GAP). "Obama made no reference to restricting the law, or any type of enforcement against whistleblowers."

"It seems he is saying exactly what a good politician and president should say," argues Kathryn Bolkovac, who exposed human trafficking in Bosnia while serving on the UN Police Task Force (and inspired the movie *The Whistleblower*). "I am sure it will at times limit his authority, as it should when a conflict of interest may arise regarding executive officials who could potentially be involved, but I see that as a positive."

The new law could help whistleblowers like Bolkovac, who was fired for her disclosures, by creating safe channels for police officers stationed in United Nations peacekeeping areas who report on illegal activity. (Bolkvoac does acknowledge, however, that "private corporations like the one who employed me still have ways of intimidating their employees.") According to GAP, the law will affect about 12 million contractors and will work to protect the $1.9 trillion spent every year on outsourcing. Nonfederal workers can already file lawsuits on behalf of the government, but this law would permanently extend protections to all employees of defense contractors and subcontractors (and temporarily for other contractors, as part of a pilot program).

One thing the law doesn't do, however, is extend those same rights to contractors in the intelligence community, an exclusion that Devine calls "inexcusable."

Radack says that the continued exclusion of the intelligence community from whistleblower protections, in addition to the president's signing statement, demonstrates that "Obama is still giving whistleblowers baby pats on the head while screwing us on the other side."

But Canterbury says it's still "not definitively clear" yet what the impact of Obama's signing statement will be. "It's going to be incredibly important for Congress to conduct rigorous oversight to ensure the law is not weakened," she says.

FBI Revamping Whistleblower Rules

By Devlin Barrett
The Wall Street Journal, October 22, 2014

WASHINGTON—The Federal Bureau of Investigation is revamping its whistleblower rules to make it easier—and potentially lucrative—for agents and employees to report misconduct within the agency, according to a federal law-enforcement official.

The changes, which include expanding the list of those eligible to receive a complaint and making whistleblowers potentially able to receive compensation, are designed to ensure complaints get processed and decided promptly and fairly, the official said.

The rules come amid a renewed debate about how best to protect whistleblowers who work at U.S. intelligence agencies—an issue that has found new urgency in the wake of National Security Agency contractor Edward Snowden's release of classified documents showing the extent of U.S. surveillance.

The new rules stem from a presidential directive issued in 2012 designed to improve protection of whistleblowers who work at intelligence agencies.

Sen. Charles Grassley (R., Iowa) has long complained the FBI mishandles whistleblower cases, accusing it of punishing people who report misconduct and failing to properly investigate allegations of wrongdoing. On Thursday, he said some of the changes outlined by the Justice Department could help.

"Nobody's got on rose-colored glasses that the culture for whistleblowers at the FBI will change anytime soon, but many of the items outlined in the FBI's analysis are promising," he said in a statement. "In an agency with so much focus on the chain of command, it makes no sense for the FBI to be the only agency in the federal government not to protect disclosures of waste, fraud, and abuse to immediate supervisors."

The FBI didn't immediately comment on the revamp.

The changes include expanding the list of FBI officials to whom a whistleblower can report concerns, the official said. Previously, a whistleblower could make a protected disclosure to the head of the office where he or she works. Under the new rules, a whistleblower can report to either the head of the office or the second tier of bosses in that office.

Whistleblowers also would be eligible for compensation if their allegations prove accurate, though how that payment system would work is unclear, the person said.

And whistleblowers would be able to use a mediation program to resolve workplace disputes if they request it, the official said.

The FBI also will give whistleblowers equal access to witnesses, if their cases lead to hearings or depositions, the official said. Those who have filed whistleblower complaints in the past haven't had the same freedom to call witnesses. Previously, FBI management has been allowed to call former employees as witnesses, while the whistleblower hasn't had the authority to require testimony from ex-FBI personnel.

The rule changes were put together by a multi-agency working group, the official said. Some of the new policies already are in effect, while others are being implemented.

In an effort to improve transparency, the bureau will also publish annual reports on whistleblower cases, the official said.

The Central Intelligence Agency has already made changes to its whistleblower policies as a result of the 2012 presidential directive, an agency spokesman said.

Patriot Games: The Odds Are Stacked Against Whistleblower Snowden

By Ashley Savage
The Conversation, July 5, 2013

The debate about whether Edward Snowden is a public interest whistleblower—the "Paul Revere" of the digital age, as his father and lawyer have dubbed him, or a "traitor," as former vice-president Dick Cheney (and a number of other US luminaries) have damned him—has taken on a new intensity.

While Snowden himself remains out of sight—last seen in the transit lounge of Moscow's Sheremetyevo International Airport—the rest of the world has argued the toss about whether, as Ban Ki Moon told the foreign affairs committee of the Icelandic parliament in Reykjavik this week, the young man had "misused" digital communications, whether he had bravely acted out of public interest or whether his actions could be classed as espionage.

To answer this question, it's instructive to focus on the nature of the offenses alleged against him. Snowden is currently charged with two offenses under the Espionage Act and a further offense of theft of government property.

The Act was passed in 1917 following the United States' entry into the Great War and despite amendments in 1921, has survived, partly due to its use as a powerful deterrent in the Cold War and partly due to the relatively few prosecutions for unauthorized leaking. However, since the Obama administration came into office, charges made against current or former public servants for offenses under the Espionage Act are increasing. Snowden becomes the eighth person to be charged and there is potential for further charges to be brought as the situation progresses.

What Do The Laws Say?

The first offense contained in section 793 (d) concerns the "Unauthorized Communication of National Defense Information". It requires the possessor to have "reason to believe that [the disclosure] is to be used to the injury of the United States or to the advantage of any foreign nation."

The second offense, concerns the "Willful Communication of Classified Communications Intelligence Information to an Unauthorized Person." Section 798 (a) (3) criminalizes unauthorized disclosures including the publication or use of

Ashley Savage, Northumbria University, Newcastle. Published under a Creative Common license by The Conversation (5 July 2013). theconversation.com information "in any manner prejudicial to the safety or interest of the United States or for the benefit of any foreign government to the detriment of the United States."

While both offenses are aimed at capturing acts of spying, both also contain elements relating to disclosures which may be harmful to the United States. The sections are deliberately open to wide interpretation, extending beyond risks of physical harm to also prosecute disclosures harmful to reputation.

The effect is that while those spying for a foreign power are easily caught, whistleblowers who make the difficult choice of bringing public attention to acts of wrongdoing can easily be dealt with by the same provisions. The sections fail to allow for consideration of the public interest benefit of any disclosures made, a deficiency which is further compounded by the lack of an available public interest defense.

What Are the Precedents?

Parallels and distinctions may be drawn between Snowden and recent disclosures by Tom Drake and Bradley Manning. Drake was a senior official in the National Security Agency. He disagreed with the Agency's decision to choose a data collection program that had a higher cost and was more intrusive to privacy than an alternative. Drake chose to escalate his concerns through official channels, approaching his superiors in the first instance before turning to the NSA Inspector General, the person tasked with oversight of agency activities.

After being dissatisfied with the response he then chose to approach the Department of Defense Inspector General before going to both the House and Senate Committees on intelligence. Still unsatisfied, he took his story to the *Baltimore Sun* and was promptly charged under the Espionage Act. Drake secured a deal with the prosecution to plead guilty for the misdemeanour offense of "wilful retention of classified information."

In contrast, Private Bradley Manning the US Army intelligence analyst chose to disclose thousands of documents to the online outlet Wikileaks. The disclosures relate to activities by the US military in Iraq and Afghanistan as well as diplomatic cables. Manning has pleaded guilty to 10 of 22 charges relating to a range of offenses and court martial proceedings are ongoing. One of the contested charges concerns the Espionage Act.

As with Manning, from available news reporting, it would appear that Snowden did not attempt to raise his concerns using official channels. One must ask why individuals are choosing to bypass available mechanisms to take the risk of going public. The Drake example may provide an indicator that the accountability mechanisms that are in place may be mistrusted at best, ineffective at worst.

Whistleblowers Now at Risk

Questions must also be raised about available whistleblowing protections. Whilst the Obama administration supported much needed reforms to the Whistleblower Protection Enhancement Act, which passed at the end of 2012, whistleblowers in the US intelligence community were excluded from the provisions. Instead, Obama signed an executive order to require agencies to establish new internal procedures and to protect against reprisals. Legislative reforms to the Military Whistleblowers Protection Act have also been tabled.

While these are positive steps, the number of high-profile unauthorized disclosures suggest the need for a detailed forensic review into the accountability mechanisms and protections available.

35 Years for Manning, and Time for Better Whistleblowing Laws

By Ashley Savage
The Conversation, August 21, 2013

Bradley Manning, the whistleblower behind the biggest leak of military secrets in history, has been sentenced to 35 years imprisonment. Convicted for six offenses under the Espionage Act, he will have his military grade reduced to the rank of Private E1, be dishonorably discharged from the Army and will lose all pay and allowances.

The reaction of to the verdict is likely to be divisive. To some Manning will remain a hero, the whistleblower who stood up to the United States and paid a heavy price for doing so. To others he will be portrayed as a traitor, a danger to national security who should have suffered a far worse punishment than the 35 years suggests.

The reason for such polarized opinion is due in part to the way his disclosures were made. Manning, of course, did not take the route of leaking his information to a traditional journalist. Instead he used an online platform. While a traditional print journalist may have exercised a level of prior restraint, the Wikileaks organization chose to release some of the leaked documents in a "raw" and unredacted form. Thousands of documents were therefore made available for the world to see, whether friend or foe.

The Manning episode also identifies the differences in editorial approach; *The Guardian* chose to report on the documents, yet declined the opportunity to republish the documents in full on the grounds of security. The option to resort to traditional methods of leaking to a journalist remains; however the recent events surrounding Edward Snowden, Glenn Greenwald, and [Greenwald's] partner David Miranda identify the difficulties in handling journalistic source material when it is placed in the jurisdiction of a NATO ally.

Those faced with few options and an overriding desire to make their concerns known are likely to resort to the internet as the fastest and surest way of disclosure.

New Era Of Online Leaking

The Manning situation is not likely to be a one-off event. Instead it should be indicative of a turning point that will lead to a new era of online leaking. Unauthorised disclosures using the internet can be seen as particularly advantageous to

Ashley Savage, Northumbria University, Newcastle. Published under a Creative Common license by The Conversation (21 August 2013). theconversation.com prospective whistleblowers. The internet provides a platform for the swift dissemination of material and can even provide a layer of anonymity.

Manning situation—and now the Snowden revelations—identify that whistleblowing can engage different legal jurisdictions around the globe. The traditional legal methods used to deter and prosecute individuals for unauthorized leaking are out of date. The actions of those motivated to use the somewhat rusty and blunt legal instruments at their disposal have succeeded in prosecuting Manning.

However, the Snowden episode shows would-be whistleblowers may use the global stage to their advantage by seeking asylum in another jurisdiction. With a degree of legal knowledge, the information and the whistleblower can transverse borders with relative ease.

Advances in modern technology identify that whistleblowing organizations can be set up in legal jurisdictions with good shield law protections for journalists, meaning the journalists cannot be coerced into giving up their source. Or they can be mobile and move from jurisdiction to jurisdiction. Whistleblowers can seek protection in countries that do not have extradition agreements in place or do not have working relationships with the aggrieved jurisdiction to which the individual had originally fled. Regardless of the eventual outcome, unauthorized disclosures of this nature can pose an underlying risk for both the individual concerned and for the national security of the nation at issue.

Better Reporting Mechanisms Needed

In the aftermath of the Manning trial, it is unlikely that legal reforms could ever outpace technological advancements. Governments must seek to provide viable authorized reporting mechanisms if they are ever going to provide a realistic alternative to unauthorized leaking. The first question the US government should ask—and one which should be considered in forensic detail—is why did Manning choose to leak the documents?

The Military Whistleblowers Protection Act 1988 exists to shield whistleblowers from retaliation if they raise concerns to Congress, an Inspector General or a person designated to receive concerns. One must question whether there are issues with the internal culture of the military which act as a deterrence to use these channels. Despite looking good on paper, the law is seldom used and has been previously labeled by Tom Devine, legal director of the Government Accountability Project, as affording "weak and nonexistent rights."

Military whistleblowers were also excluded from the Whistleblower Protection Enhancement Act 2012, which provided much-needed reform to protections afforded to Civil Service whistleblowers but excluded those in the military and intelligence community.

Proposed reforms aimed at enhancing the existing protections are currently before a Congressional committee. Even if these aims succeed into law, they cannot be relied upon to deter unauthorized leaking without clear moves to address the internal culture in the armed forces.

As Daniel Ellsberg, who famously leaked the Pentagon Papers, commented in response to the sentencing verdict, "Manning's 35-year sentence will not deter all future whistleblowers." Providing them with authorized channels which create less risk to a whistleblower's employment position and to their liberty, as well as addressing the risks associated with leaking national security material, may go some way to satisfy the opinions of those on both sides of the fence.

G20 Still Has a Way to Go with Whistleblower Protections

By Suelette Dreyfus
The Conversation, June 19, 2014

The G20 countries' whistleblower protection laws fail to meet best international standards, according to the first independent evaluation of both public and private sector whistleblowing laws.

This is despite the fact that in 2010, these countries—the largest economies in the world—pledged adequate measures would be in place to protect whistleblowers, and provide them with safe, reliable reporting avenues for revealing corruption, fraud and other crimes.

Many G20 countries have large gaps that leave whistleblowers with little legal recourse to be reinstated or compensated if they are sacked for exposing wrongdoing. Corruption increases costs for businesses and causes the loss of billions of dollars in economic activity.

Whistleblowing is possibly the most effective way to expose corruption, fraud and other wrongdoing. Hospitals are better, cars are safer and taxes are spent more wisely—thanks to whistleblowers.

Without strong whistleblower laws, employees are subject to harassment, firing, physical threats and other types of retaliation. This deters people from reporting information that could save lives, environmental resources or money.

Private Sector Lagging

Researched by an international team of experts from both civil society and academia, the report was launched jointly this week in Paris at the OECD (Organization for Economic Cooperation and Development), in Brisbane at an anti-corruption conference, and in Melbourne at the C20 (Civil Society) Conference.

It scores the G20 countries' laws (with a 1 for comprehensive, 2 for somewhat or partially comprehensive or 3 for absent/not at all comprehensive) across a range of criteria for the protection of whistleblowers, and includes comparison tables for public and private sector laws.

The report shows that the private sector protections lag well behind the protections applying in the public sector in most G20 countries. The report results mean that the G20 should make addressing this shortcoming a strategic priority when

Suelette Dreyfus, University of Melbourne. Published under a Creative Common license by The Conversation (19 June 2014). theconversation.com they meet in Brisbane in November. Reform to the public sector protection laws must also stay on the agenda because while these have improved a great deal, these laws also fall short of best standards.

However it's not all doom and gloom. Since 2010, new whistleblower laws have been passed in Australia, Bosnia and Herzegovina, France, India, Italy, Jamaica, Kosovo, Luxembourg, Malaysia, Malta, Peru, Slovenia, the Republic of Korea, Uganda, the US and Zambia. Dozens of other countries are considering new laws or monitoring how their current laws are functioning in practice.

Many elements of public and private sector laws in most G20 countries now reflect international best practice. These include protections from a wide range of retaliation, a broad definition of who can qualify as a "whistleblower," and options to report internally or to government regulators. Further, most laws require employees to have a reasonable belief—not definitive proof—that a disclosure is accurate.

Progressing, but Improvement Needed

Meaningful progress has occurred in the whistleblower laws of several G20 countries, notably China, France, India, the Republic of Korea, Australia and the United States.

But the report highlights at least four key areas in need of improvement across both sectors:

1. Protection for using external disclosure avenues when justified and required, such as the media, Members of Parliament, non-government organisations and labor unions

2. Improved protections for employees making anonymous reports of wrongdoing

3. Requiring organisations to have good internal disclosure procedures (e.g., including requirements to establish reporting channels, internal investigation procedures, and to protect internal whistleblowers from point of disclosure)

4. Requiring transparency and accountability on use of the legislation/availability of protection, including annual reporting and overriding of confidentiality clauses.

Anonymous channels are critical to get those who know about corruption to speak up to someone in the first instance. Without them, a government institution or a corporation may never know about wrongdoing.

Technology can enable things like anonymous and confidential reporting of fraud and corruption in ways that were not possible previously. However, people must also be confident that management will actually act in good faith in the disclosures. Without that, a company can install the best identity-hiding, military-grade encryption systems in the world - but whistleblowers won't use it. They will be loath to step forward to reveal the truth about serious wrongdoing.

In their current G20 Anti-Corruption Action Plan (2013 – 2014), the G20 leaders committed to:

. . . enact and implement whistleblower protection rules. . . and also take specific actions. . . to ensure that those reporting on corruption, including journalists, can exercise their function without fear of any harassment or threat or of private or government legal action for reporting in good faith.

They have not yet achieved this goal.

Making laws that truly protect whistleblowers requires some skill and specialist knowledge but it can be done, as evidenced by the progress made so far. What's missing in many G20 countries isn't lawyerly expertise; it's political will. Hopefully leaders at November's G20 meeting will commit to finding this will.

Today, the consulting work has dried up. He has run out of money and thinks he is about a month from being homeless.

"I served my country for 23 years. I could go get a job for $10 at Wal-Mart," he said. "But that's not the issue, the issue is, where's my money?"

Despite efforts by senators and various legislative committees to get him compensated for his loss, the issue has never been resolved, for political and bureaucratic reasons.

He thinks part of the problem is that there's no structure to compensate whistleblowers in the intelligence field. He also says that the Obama administration has criminalized whistleblowing on levels he's never seen before.

Today, he spends his days in the wilderness, fly-fishing and bird hunting with his dogs.

The Advocate

It's 8 a.m. on the 11th floor of a K Street office building, and Jesselyn Radack, 42, is trying to tame her curly blond hair with a straightening iron.

"Our PR people said, 'Straight hair is serious hair,'" she said, laughing. "But it is like 100 degrees outside."

Radack is an attorney and former ethics adviser for the Justice Department. Her supervisor told her to find another job after she disclosed after Sept. 11 that the FBI interrogated John Walker Lindh, known as the "American Taliban," without an attorney present. Her case was closed in 2003, and prosecutors never identified a potential charge against her.

Today, Radack is a mother of three and director of national security and human rights at the Government Accountability Project, a whistleblowing advocacy organization.

That means she's an advocate, attorney and, it turns out, therapist of sorts for whistleblowers who come to her "bankrupt, blacklisted and broken," she says.

"Once you are labeled that way, you are just radioactive," she said.

And she can certainly empathize.

Before she decided to make her disclosure, she says she suffered from horrible insomnia. She also has long suffered from multiple sclerosis, and the stress caused flare-ups of her disease.

"I had this knowledge and had to do something," she said on a recent afternoon at her brick home in Tenleytown. "After law school, I thought the government wears the white hat and is on the right side of the law. I never expected to be a whistleblower."

But the Yale Law School graduate saw something she thought was wrong and felt compelled to report it.

After her case went public, she noticed a chill in how she and her family were treated. She took her children to the "tot shabbat," or sabbath celebration for young children, at Temple Sinai in northwest Washington and noticed that no one would sit near her and her family. It turns out that some of the people she blew the whistle on also attended her temple. The situation got so bad, she said, she had to talk to the rabbi about it.

"We're inside the Beltway, and it's a small city," Radack says. "It's like high school. They just freeze you out."

The Fraud Behind a $14 Million Whistleblower Award

By Jean Eaglesham
The Wall Street Journal, February 27, 2014

A record $14 million whistleblower award paid by the Securities and Exchange Commission last year was for a tip about an alleged Chicago-based scheme to defraud foreign investors seeking U.S. residency, according to people familiar with the payment.

The award is by far the biggest arising from a 2010 law designed in part to encourage tipsters to come forward with information about financial fraud. The SEC announced the payment in October without naming the whistleblower or the case, as the law gives tipsters the option to remain anonymous.

The SEC's whistleblower program, established under the Dodd-Frank financial-overhaul law, has yet to produce many payouts: The agency has paid a total of about $225,000 in five other awards since the program became operational in August 2011, according to the SEC.

"We're confident there will be more frequent and numerous payouts as the program continues to gain momentum," said SEC enforcement chief Andrew Ceresney in a statement.

The case that led to the $14 million-plus payment centers on allegations last year that about 250 investors, mostly Chinese, were "duped" by 30-year-old Anshoo R. Sethi and his two Chicago, Illinois-based companies into paying a total of more than $155 million for a supposed plan to build a hotel and conference center, said the people familiar with the matter. The SEC said the investors were led to believe they were boosting their chances of green cards, because the scheme was designed to qualify for an immigration program that offers U.S. residency for job-creating investments.

In fact, the agency alleged, Mr. Sethi and his companies lacked the necessary building permits, their claims to have the support of major hotel chains were false and the documentation they gave to the immigration authorities was "phony."

A lawyer representing Mr. Sethi and his companies declined to comment, and an SEC spokesman declined to comment on the award.

The SEC program is among several government mechanisms for making payments to those who help identify frauds. In 2012, the Internal Revenue Service paid former UBS AG banker Bradley Birkenfeld $104 million for providing prosecutors with evidence about the firm's efforts to promote tax evasion. That is believed to be the largest whistleblower award paid by the U.S. government to an individual.

Before 2010, the SEC had a whistleblower program that was limited to insider trading and had been criticized by lawmakers for paying relatively few awards.

The agency has received more than 6,500 whistleblower tips since the revamped program began, according to SEC figures.

The SEC's Mr. Ceresney said in the statement that the agency is "encouraged by the success reflected in the whistleblower payouts" made so far.

The SEC brought civil charges against Mr. Sethi in February 2013. In April, a federal court ordered the return to the investors of $147 million, which was being held on their behalf in U.S. bank accounts. Mr. Sethi and his companies agreed to return the funds, according to court filings.

The SEC is continuing its enforcement action over $11 million of "administrative fees" paid by investors, most of which the agency alleged has been misappropriated. Settlement talks to resolve the case are continuing, according to court filings.

The SEC decided the whistleblower deserved 10% of the $147 million returned to investors, the bottom of the range established by the program, according to the people familiar with the matter. Tipsters who lead to a successful enforcement action, with SEC sanctions of more than $1 million, can receive as much as 30% of the money collected.

The SEC's new rules allow the agency to make awards based on any money "ordered to be paid" in an enforcement action. Paying a whistleblower based on the return of investors' frozen funds "shows how aggressive the SEC is willing to be in applying its rules to make awards," said Christian Bartholomew, a former SEC trial lawyer and now a partner at law firm Weil, Gotshal & Manges LLP.

SEC officials say if a tip leads to a new investigation, it typically takes two or more years for that probe to be concluded. Even if there is an enforcement action with sanctions of more than $1 million, it is likely to take several more months for the whistleblower claim to be approved.

"It's rare to get the perfect whistleblower—someone in the belly of the beast, who provides a previously unknown blueprint to a fraud that falls within the SEC's jurisdiction," said Thomas Sporkin, a partner at law firm BuckleySandler LLP and former head of the SEC's office of market intelligence.

An SEC spokesman declined to say how many of the tips have led to investigations, or give details on how many claims for awards have been submitted and rejected.

But the new figures for a whistleblower program run by the Commodity Futures Trading Commission offer a peek into some of the reasons awards may be denied.

The CFTC has received 255 tips and 55 claims for awards under its whistleblower program, set up under the same law as the SEC scheme. All 25 of the whistleblower award applications the regulator has ruled on to date have been rejected, according to CFTC figures.

Some were denied because the tip was first made before the July 2010 legal start date. Other claims failed because the information didn't lead to a successful

After the Whistle:
Revealers of Government Secrets Share
How Their Lives Have Changed

By Emily Wax
The Washington Post, July 28, 2013

The former high-ranking National Security Agency analyst now sells iPhones. The top intelligence officer at the CIA lives in a motor home outside Yellowstone National Park and spends his days fly-fishing for trout. The FBI translator fled Washington for the West Coast.

This is what life looks like for some after revealing government secrets. Blowing the whistle on wrongdoing, according to those who did it. Jeopardizing national security, according to the government.

Heroes. Scofflaws. They're all people who had to get on with their lives.

Edward Snowden eventually will. The former NSA contractor who leaked classified documents on U.S. surveillance programs is now in Russia, with his fate in limbo. The Justice Department announced last week that it won't seek the death penalty in prosecuting him, but he is still charged with theft and espionage.

Say he makes it out of there. What next, beyond the pending charges? What happens to people who make public things that the government wanted to keep secret?

A look at the lives of a handful of those who did just that shows that they often wind up far from the stable government jobs they held. They can even wind up in the aisles of a craft store.

Peter Van Buren, a veteran Foreign Service officer who blew the whistle on waste and mismanagement of the Iraq reconstruction program, most recently found himself working at a local arts and crafts store and learned a lot about "glitter and the American art of scrapbooking."

"What happens when you are thrown out of the government and blacklisted is that you lose your security clearance and it's very difficult to find a grown-up job in Washington," said Van Buren, who lives in Falls Church and wrote the book *We Meant Well: How I Helped Lose the Battle for the Hearts and Minds of the Iraqi People*. "Then, you have to step down a few levels to find a place where they don't care enough about your background to even look into why you washed up there."

The Apple Store Employee

"Let's sit in the back," Thomas Drake says when choosing a booth at Parker's Classic American Restaurant in downtown Bethesda during his lunch break from Apple. "I have a lot to say. I was a public servant. That's a very high honor. It's supposed to mean something."

Drake was prosecuted under the World War I–era Espionage Act for mishandling national defense information.

His alleged crime: voicing concerns to superiors after the Sept. 11, 2001, attacks about violations of Americans' privacy by the nation's largest intelligence organization (the NSA) and later, in frustration, speaking to a reporter about waste and fraud in the NSA intelligence program. (He says he revealed no classified information.)

He lost his $155,000-a-year job and pension, even though in 2011 the criminal case against him fell apart. The former top spokesman for the Justice Department, Matthew Miller, later said the case against Drake may have been an "ill-considered choice for prosecution."

Drake, now 56, is tall and lanky and dresses as though he's ready, at any moment, to go on a gentle hike. He is the type of person who likes consistency. He went to work at Apple the day after the charges against him were dropped, surprising his co-workers who thought he would at least take a day off. In 2010, he got an adjunct professor job at Strayer University but was fired soon after, he says, while he was under government investigation.

"I was just blacklisted," he said, adding that he started his own company but has only had minor work. "People were afraid to deal with a federal government whistleblower."

Drake long planned to be a career public servant. He enlisted in the Air Force in 1979 and flew on spy planes and once was a CIA analyst and an expert in electronic intelligence missions. On Sept. 11, 2001, he reported for his first day of work as a senior executive at the NSA's Fort Meade campus, and shortly thereafter, he voiced "the gravest of concerns" regarding a secret domestic surveillance program that, he says, was launched shortly after the attacks.

In 2006, he was reassigned from the NSA to be a professor at the National Defense University, but he was forced to leave in 2007 when his security clearance was suspended.

Ironically, he was teaching a class called "The Secret Side of U.S. History."

Now working at the Apple Store and living in Howard County, he is extremely grateful for his hourly wage retail job. He has no choice. He has massive legal debts and a son ready to go to college.

Last year, he was working when he spotted an unlikely customer: Attorney General Eric H. Holder Jr., who came in to check out iPhones.

Drake introduced himself and asked: "Do you know why they have come after me?"

"Yes, I do," Holder said.

"But do you know the rest of the story?," he asked.

Holder quickly left with his security detail, Drake said.

"It's not every day you get to talk to the chief law enforcement officer of the land about your case," Drake said, "or at least try."

The Author in Oregon

Sometimes Washington is just the last place you can stand to be.

Sibel Edmonds was once described by the American Civil Liberties Union as "the most gagged person in the history of the United States." And she was a regular on Washington's protest circuit.

She was fired from her work as a translator at the FBI for trying to expose security breaches and cover-ups that she thought presented a danger to U.S. security. Her allegations were supported and confirmed by the Justice Department's inspector general office and bipartisan congressional investigations, but she was not offered her job back.

She also published a memoir, *Classified Woman—The Sibel Edmonds Story.*

Then last summer, Edmonds, 43, decamped with her 5-year-old daughter and husband to Bend, Oregon, which is known as the sunny side of the state. The July weather is 77 degrees without humidity, and there are 33 independently owned coffee shops and nine microbreweries.

"I am touring every single one. Plus, we don't even have air conditioning here," she said. "We open the windows and feel the breeze."

For years before she left, Edmonds found Washington's atmosphere suffocating. Many of her neighbors in Alexandria were lobbyists and contractors, who, she says stopped talking to her after her name appeared in the newspaper.

Luckily, her husband of 21 years is a retail consultant and can live anywhere. She says that most whistleblowers have spouses who work in the same agencies, which typically puts pressure on their marriages.

She is still dedicated, she says, to the cause of exposing injustice and making information free. She spends hours running "Boiling Frog Post: Home of the Irate Minority," a podcast and Web site that covers whistleblowing and tries to create broader exposure for revelations. She is also founder and director of the National Security Whistleblowers Coalition.

"I think in the current climate, Congress and Washington is a last resort," she said. "We are going directly to the people and focused on releasing information. And I don't have to do that from Washington."

The Alienated Fly Fisherman

"The connection is really bad, it must be the NSA surveillance program," Richard Barlow says jokingly when speaking to a reporter on his cellphone from his motor home outside Yellowstone National Park.

"I'm out here with the grizzly bears," he says. "But this is where I'm comfortable. I'm a 58-year-old seriously damaged, burned-out intelligence officer."

Barlow says he suffers from chronic PTSD, which makes it hard for him to deal with stress and sometimes other people. He finds comfort in his three dogs: Sassy, Prairie and Spirit.

His supporters say that shouldn't be surprising considering what he went through.

Barlow started his career as a rising star tasked with organizing efforts to target Pakistan's clandestine networks for acquiring nuclear materiel. He won the CIA's Exceptional Accomplishment Award in 1988 for work that led to arrests, including that of Pakistani nuclear scientist A.Q. Khan.

He testified before Congress under direct orders from his CIA superiors, but he says he later became the target of criticism from some people in the CIA who were supporting the mujahideen (including Osama bin Laden at the time) in efforts to push the Soviets out of Afghanistan.

He says he chose to leave the CIA, and in early 1989, he went to work as the first weapons-of-mass-destruction intelligence officer in the administration of President George H.W. Bush. Barlow continued to write assessments of Pakistan's nuclear weapons program for then–Defense Secretary Dick Cheney. He concluded that Pakistan already possessed nuclear weapons, had modified its F-16s to deliver these weapons and had continued to violate U.S. laws.

The intelligence would have legally precluded a sale of $1.4 billion worth of additional F-16s to Pakistan.

But in August 1989, Barlow learned that the Defense Department had asserted that the F-16s were not capable of delivering Pakistan's nuclear weapons. Barlow said that Congress was being lied to, and he objected internally.

Days later, he was fired.

"Back then I was disgustingly patriotic and I thought the government is allowing Pakistan to develop and spread nuclear weapons and I got destroyed for trying to stop it," he said.

He was 35 at the time. His marriage to his 29-year-old wife, who also worked at the CIA, was shattered.

After a 1993 probe, the inspector general at the State Department and the CIA concluded that Barlow had been fired as a reprisal. The Defense Department maintained that the Pentagon was within its rights to fire Barlow. A 1997 GAO report largely vindicated Barlow, and his security clearances were restored. But, he says, he was unable to get rehired permanently by the government because his record was smeared.

He eventually found some work as a consultant, helping to start and run the FBI's counterproliferation program out of Sandia National Laboratories.

Meanwhile, he has been trying for years to collect the $89,500 annual pension and health insurance that he thinks he is owed.

Much of what he tried to report about Pakistan's nuclear program is common knowledge today, and several national security bestsellers have included his story, including George Crile III's 2003 book *Charlie Wilson's War: The Extraordinary Story of the Largest Covert Operation in History*, which describes Barlow as a "brilliant young analyst who gave devastating testimony."

Today, the consulting work has dried up. He has run out of money and thinks he is about a month from being homeless.

"I served my country for 23 years. I could go get a job for $10 at Wal-Mart," he said. "But that's not the issue, the issue is, where's my money?"

Despite efforts by senators and various legislative committees to get him compensated for his loss, the issue has never been resolved, for political and bureaucratic reasons.

He thinks part of the problem is that there's no structure to compensate whistle-blowers in the intelligence field. He also says that the Obama administration has criminalized whistleblowing on levels he's never seen before.

Today, he spends his days in the wilderness, fly-fishing and bird hunting with his dogs.

The Advocate

It's 8 a.m. on the 11th floor of a K Street office building, and Jesselyn Radack, 42, is trying to tame her curly blond hair with a straightening iron.

"Our PR people said, 'Straight hair is serious hair,'" she said, laughing. "But it is like 100 degrees outside."

Radack is an attorney and former ethics adviser for the Justice Department. Her supervisor told her to find another job after she disclosed after Sept. 11 that the FBI interrogated John Walker Lindh, known as the "American Taliban," without an attorney present. Her case was closed in 2003, and prosecutors never identified a potential charge against her.

Today, Radack is a mother of three and director of national security and human rights at the Government Accountability Project, a whistleblowing advocacy organization.

That means she's an advocate, attorney and, it turns out, therapist of sorts for whistleblowers who come to her "bankrupt, blacklisted and broken," she says.

"Once you are labeled that way, you are just radioactive," she said.

And she can certainly empathize.

Before she decided to make her disclosure, she says she suffered from horrible insomnia. She also has long suffered from multiple sclerosis, and the stress caused flare-ups of her disease.

"I had this knowledge and had to do something," she said on a recent afternoon at her brick home in Tenleytown. "After law school, I thought the government wears the white hat and is on the right side of the law. I never expected to be a whistle-blower."

But the Yale Law School graduate saw something she thought was wrong and felt compelled to report it.

After her case went public, she noticed a chill in how she and her family were treated. She took her children to the "tot shabbat," or sabbath celebration for young children, at Temple Sinai in northwest Washington and noticed that no one would sit near her and her family. It turns out that some of the people she blew the whistle on also attended her temple. The situation got so bad, she said, she had to talk to the rabbi about it.

"We're inside the Beltway, and it's a small city," Radack says. "It's like high school. They just freeze you out."

enforcement action or was provided under compulsion, rather than voluntarily as the award rules require. Another 30 claims are awaiting a decision, the new CFTC figures show. A spokeswoman for the CFTC declined to comment.

One Whistleblower Gets $30 Million in the Bank, but Others Count the Personal Cost

By Jana Kasperkevic
The Guardian, September 23, 2014

This week, the Securities and Exchange Commission made history by promising an anonymous overseas whistleblower a reward of $30 million.

It doesn't usually work out that way for whistleblowers. Ringing the bell on abuse in a company or government usually means losing jobs and status. The norm is pariah treatment and low-wage jobs, as well as trips to the welfare office and the lingering threat of prosecution or intimidation.

Consider: it's not every day that you get to buy an iPhone from an ex-NSA officer. Yet a number of people visiting the Washington metro-area Apple store get to do just that. For over a year now, several days a week Thomas Drake puts on his blue Apple work T-shirt and goes to work.

Drake, former senior executive at National Security Agency, is well known in the national security circles. In 2006, he leaked information about the NSA's Trailblazer project to *Baltimore Sun.* Years later, in 2010, he was prosecuted under the Espionage Act, but the government ended up dropping all 10 felony charges against him. He pleaded guilty to a misdemeanor charge for unauthorized use of a computer.

Drake, unlike other NSA whistleblowers, has the freedom to move freely within any city or state within America. His freedom, however, comes with a very tangible price: his livelihood.

"You have to mortgage your house, you have to empty your bank account. I went from making well over $150,000 a year to a quarter of that," Drake says in *Silenced,* a recently released documentary depicting the lives of several national security whistleblowers. *Silenced,* which made its debut at the Tribeca Film Festival, is to be screened at additional movie festivals this fall. "The cost alone, financially—never mind the personal cost—is approaching a million dollars in terms of lost income, expenses and other costs I incurred."

"Obviously, I am a *persona non grata* within the government. . . and so I am unemployed," Drake says to the cameras in *Silenced.* "I did look for work. I spent a lot of time looking for work. I applied for a part-time position with Apple, and several months later I actually got a phone call. I ended up working at an Applestore in the metro DC area as an expert."

This kind of result is what most whistleblowers can expect. The potential threat of prosecution, the mounting legal bills and the lack of future job opportunities all contribute to a hesitation among many to rock the boat.

President Obama has approved legislation to help protect federal whistleblowers against retaliation and economic ruin. In November 2012, Obama signed the Whistleblower Protection Enhancement Act into law, which was to expand whistleblower protections available to corporate whistleblowers to federal workers.

Yet whistleblowers have been left on their own to struggle with the consequences of going public.

Jesselyn Radack says whistleblowers need better protections. She is a former Justice Department ethics attorney and whistleblower who went on to defend Drake and Kiriakou. She is currently one of Edward Snowden's lawyers.

"The Whistleblower Protection Enhancement Act. . . has a big loophole that covers national security and intelligence officials, people exactly like Tom Drake at the NSA, Edward Snowden at NSA, and John Kiriakou at CIA, Steven Kim at the State Department, Jeffrey Sterling at the CIA, Peter van Buren, who was at the State Department—the people that I would argue we most need to hear from and want to hear from," says Radack, noting that Obama's order applies only to employees—not to contractors such as Edward Snowden.

Finance whistleblowers can, theoretically, collect awards ranging from $300,000 to $104m for disclosing secrets about their employers cheating on taxes and violating securities law. Activist investor Bill Ackman offered a $250,000-per-year-for-10-years deal to an employee of Herbalife for supporting Ackman's thesis that the company fools its workers and customers. The company and other hedge fund managers, including Carl Icahn, dispute Ackman's remarks.

The price of leaking national security problems, in particular, is steep. National security whistleblowers have no prospect of financial rewards.

Kiriakou, a former CIA analyst, became the first former government official to confirm the use of waterboarding against al-Qaida suspects in 2009. Three years later, in 2012, he was prosecuted for leaking classified information under the Espionage Act. After he was accused of violating the Espionage Act, Kiriakou had to look for employment outside the field of national security.

"I have applied for every job I can think of—everything from grocery stores to Toys R Us to Starbucks. You name it, I've applied there. Haven't gotten even an email or a call back," Kiriakou says at some point in the film. "I'll be honest with you, I really miss working and so regardless of what the job is, I'll be happy to just pass eight hours a day."

He was not the only one in his family to lose his job as a result of his disclosures. His wife quit her job because of threats of security investigations, says Kiriakou.

After both of them were unemployed for seven months, she informed him that they couldn't afford food for the next week. In the days to follow, they found themselves at a welfare office, where they were told they qualified for a variety of assistance including food stamps, Medicaid and job training.

The stark reality of their financial situation was enough to get Kiriakou to consider changing his plea. That, and the possibility of not seeing his children grow up.

"She doesn't make enough money to support our household. We could borrow enough for two years to keep her going," he says. "But if I am found guilty and get more than two years, I mean—we think we are ruined now?—we'd be ruined permanently after that. I want to fight it but I have kids and I just can't risk them losing me for six to twelve years."

Kiriakou is currently serving a 30-month jail sentence. Instead of telling his children that he is going to jail, Kiriakou and his wife have told them that he is going to Pennsylvania to "teach bad guys how to get their diplomas."

With Kiriakou in jail, his family continues to struggle to make ends meet.

"They are still in dire straits, living from paycheck to paycheck," Radack told the audience at the New America after recently held screening of *Silenced*. A Facebook page, *Defend John Kiriakou*, lists instructions on how to contribute to Kiriakou's commissary account. Another post invites supporters to buy him a subscription to *The New York Times*' Sunday edition. Radack already purchased him a Monday through Saturday subscription. He receives all papers two days after they are published.

"I am sitting in front of you as a free human being, I can't tell you what it means to be free," Drake told the audience after the screening. "I paid an incredibly high price."

The Next Battleground in the War on Whistleblowers

By Peter Van Buren
The Nation, March 4, 2014

The Obama administration has just opened a new front in its ongoing war on whistleblowers. It's taking its case against one man, former Transportation Security Administration (TSA) Air Marshal Robert MacLean, all the way to the Supreme Court. So hold on, because we're going back down the rabbit hole with the Most Transparent Administration ever.

Despite all the talk by Washington insiders about how whistleblowers like Edward Snowden should work through the system rather than bring their concerns directly into the public sphere, MacLean is living proof of the hell of trying to do so. Through the Supreme Court, the Department of Justice (DOJ) wants to use MacLean's case to further limit what kinds of information can qualify for statutory whistleblowing protections. If the DOJ gets its way, only information that the government thinks is appropriate—a contradiction in terms when it comes to whistleblowing—could be revealed. Such a restriction would gut the legal protections of the Whistleblower Protection Act and have a chilling effect on future acts of conscience.

Having lost its case against MacLean in the lower courts, the DOJ is seeking to win in front of the Supreme Court. If heard by the Supremes—and there's no guarantee of that—this would represent that body's first federal whistleblower case of the post–9/11 era. And if it were to rule for the government, even more information about an out-of-control executive branch will disappear under the dark umbrella of "national security."

On the other hand, should the court rule against the government, or simply turn down the case, whistleblowers like MacLean will secure a little more protection than they've had so far in the Obama years. Either way, an important message will be sent at a moment when revelations of government wrongdoing have moved from the status of obscure issue to front-page news.

The issues in the MacLean case—who is entitled to whistleblower protection, what use can be made of retroactive classification to hide previously unclassified information, how many informal classification categories the government can create bureaucratically, and what role the Constitution and the Supreme Court have in all this—are arcane and complex. But stay with me. Understanding the depths

Peter Van Buren, author of the book *We Meant Well: How I Helped Lose the Battle for the Hearts and Minds of the Iraqi People.* This article was originally published on TomDispatch.com. Reprinted with permission.

to which the government is willing to sink to punish one man who blew the whistle tells us the world about Washington these days and, as they say, the devil is in the details.

Robert MacLean, Whistleblower

MacLean's case is simple—and complicated.

Here's the simple part: MacLean was an air marshal, flying armed aboard American aircraft as the last defense against a terror attack. In July 2003, all air marshals received a briefing about a possible hijacking plot. Soon after, the TSA, which oversees the marshals, sent an unencrypted, open-air text message to their cell phones cancelling several months of missions for cost-cutting reasons. Fearing that such cancellations in the midst of a hijacking alert might create a dangerous situation for the flying public, MacLean worked his way through the system. He first brought his concerns to his supervisor and then to the Department of Homeland Security's inspector general. Each responded that nothing could be done.

After hitting a dead end, and hoping that public pressure might force the TSA to change its policy, MacLean talked anonymously to a reporter who broadcast a critical story. After eleven members of Congress pitched in, the TSA reversed itself. A year later, MacLean appeared on TV in disguise to criticize agency dress and boarding policies that he felt made it easier for passengers to recognize marshals who work undercover. (On your next flight keep an eye out for the young man in khakis with a fanny pack and a large watch, often wearing a baseball cap and eyeing boarders from a first class seat.) This time the TSA recognized MacLean's voice and discovered that he had also released the unclassified 2003 text message. He was fired in April 2006.

When MacLean contested his dismissal through internal government channels, he discovered that, months *after* firing him, the TSA had retroactively classified the text message he had leaked. Leaking classified documents is more than cause enough to fire a federal worker, and that might have been the end of it. MacLean, however, was no typical cubicle-dwelling federal employee. An Air Force veteran, he asserted his status as a protected whistleblower and has spent the last seven years marching through the system trying to get his job back.

How Everything in Government Became Classified

The text message MacLean leaked was retroactively classified as "security sensitive information" (SSI), a designation that had been around for years but whose usage the TSA only codified via memo in November 2003. When it comes to made-up classifications, that agency's set of them proved to be only one of twenty-eight known versions that now exist within the government bureaucracy. In truth, no one is sure how many varieties of pseudo-classifications even exist under those multiple policies, or how many documents they cover as there are no established reporting requirements.

By law there are officially only three levels of governmental classification: confidential, secret and top secret. Other indicators, such as NOFORN and ORCON, seen, for instance on some of the NSA documents Edward Snowden released, are called "handling instructions," although they, too, function as unofficial categories of classification. Each of the three levels of official classification has its own formal definition and criteria for use. It is theoretically possible to question the level of classification of a document. However much they may be ignored, there are standards for their declassification and various supervisors can also shift levels of classification as a final report, memo or briefing takes shape. The system is designed, at least in theory and occasionally in practice, to have some modicum of accountability and reviewability.

The government's post-9/11 desire to classify more and more information ran head on into the limits of classification as enacted by Congress. The response by various agencies was to invent a proliferation of designations like SSI that would sweep unclassified information under the umbrella of classification and confer on ever more unclassified information a (sort of) classified status. In the case of the TSA, the agency even admits on its own website that a document with an SSI stamp is unclassified, but prohibits its disclosure anyway.

Imagine the equivalent at home: you arbitrarily establish a classification called Spouse Sensitive Information that prohibits your partner from seeing the family bank statements. And if all this is starting to make no sense, then you can better understand the topsy-turvy world Robert MacLean found himself in.

MacLean Wins a Battle in Court

In 2013, after a long series of civil service and legal wrangles, the United States Court of Appeals for the Federal Circuit handed down a decision confirming the government's right to retroactively classify information. This may make some sense—if you squint hard enough from a Washington perspective. Imagine a piece of innocuous information already released that later takes on national security significance. A retroactive classification can't get the toothpaste back in the tube, but bureaucratically speaking it would at least prevent more toothpaste from being squeezed out. The same ruling, of course, could also be misused to ensnare someone like MacLean who shared unclassified information.

The court also decided that, retrospective classification or not, MacLean was indeed entitled to protection under the Whistleblower Protection Act of 1989. That act generally limits its protections to "disclosures not specifically prohibited by law," typically held to mean unclassified material. This, the court insisted, was the category MacLean fit into and so could not be fired. The court avoided the question of whether or not someone could be fired for disclosing retroactively classified information and focused on whether a made-up category like SSI was "classified" at all.

The court affirmed that laws passed by Congress creating formal classifications like "top secret" trump regulations made up by executive branch bureaucrats. In other words, as the Constitution intended, the legislative branch makes the laws and serves as a check and balance on the executive branch. Congress says what is classified and that say-so cannot be modified via an executive branch memo. One of MacLean's lawyers hailed the court's decision as restoring "enforceability for the Whistleblower Protection Act's public free speech rights. It ruled that only Congress has the authority to remove whistleblower rights. Agency-imposed restraints are not relevant for whistleblower protection rights."

The ruling made it clear that the TSA had fired MacLean in retaliation for a legally protected act of whistleblowing. He should have been offered his job back the next day.

Not a Happy Ending but a Sad New Beginning

No such luck. Instead, on January 27, 2014, the Department of Justice petitioned the Supreme Court to overturn the lower court's decision. If it has its way, the next time a troublesome whistleblower emerges, the executive need only retroactively slap a non-reviewable pseudo-classification on whatever information has been revealed and fire the employee. The department is, then, asking the Supreme Court to grant the executive branch the practical power to decide whether or not a whistleblower is entitled to legal protection. The chilling effect is obvious.

In addition, the mere fact that the DOJ is seeking to bring the case via a petition is significant. Such petitions, called writs of certiorari, or certs, ask that the Supreme Court overturn a lower court's decision. Through the cert process, the court sets its own agenda. Some 10,000 certs are submitted in a typical year. Most lack merit and are quickly set aside without comment. Typically, fewer than 100 of those 10,000 are chosen to move forward for a possibly precedent-setting decision. However, only a tiny number of all the certs filed are initiated by the government; on average, just fifteen in a Supreme Court term.

It's undoubtedly a measure of the importance the Obama administration gives to preserving secrecy above all else that it has chosen to take such an aggressive stance against MacLean—especially given the desperately low odds of success. It will be several months before we know whether the court will hear the case.

This Is War

MacLean is simply trying to get his old air marshal job back by proving he was wrongly fired for an act of whistleblowing. For the rest of us, however, this is about much more than where MacLean goes to work.

The Obama administration's attacks on whistleblowers are well documented. It has charged more of them—seven—under the Espionage Act than all past presidencies combined. In addition, it recently pressured State Department whistleblower Stephen Kim into a guilty plea (in return for a lighter sentence) by threatening him with the full force of that act. His case was even more controversial because the FBI named Fox News's James Rosen as a co-conspirator for receiving information from Kim as part of his job as a journalist. None of this is accidental, coincidental or haphazard. It's a pattern. And it's meant to be. This is war.

MacLean's case is one more battle in that war. By taking the extraordinary step of going to the Supreme Court, the executive branch wants, by fiat, to be able to turn an unclassified but embarrassing disclosure today into a prohibited act tomorrow, and then use that to get rid of an employee. They are, in essence, putting whistleblowers in the untenable position of having to predict the future. The intent is clearly to silence them before they speak on the theory that the easiest leak to stop is the one that never happens. A frightened, cowed workforce is likely to be one result; another—falling into the category of unintended consequences—might be to force more potential whistleblowers to take the Manning/Snowden path.

The case against MacLean also represents an attempt to broaden executive power in another way. At the moment, only Congress can "prohibit actions under the law," something unique to it under the Constitution. In its case against MacLean, the Justice Department seeks to establish the right of the executive and its agencies to create their own pseudo-categories of classification that can be used to prohibit actions not otherwise prohibited by law. In other words, it wants to trump Congress. Regulation made by memo would then stand above the law in prosecuting—or effectively persecuting—whistleblowers. A person of conscience like MacLean could be run out of his job by a memo.

In seeking to claim more power over whistleblowers, the executive also seeks to overturn another principle of law that goes by the term *ex post facto*. Laws are implemented on a certain day and at a certain time. Long-held practice says that one cannot be punished later for an act that was legal when it happened. Indeed, *ex post facto* criminal laws are expressly forbidden by the Constitution. This prohibition was written in direct response to the injustices of British rule at a time when Parliamentary laws could indeed criminalize actions retrospectively. While some leeway exists today in the US for *ex post facto* actions in civil cases and when it comes to sex crimes against children, the issue as it affects whistleblowers brushes heavily against the Constitution and, in a broader sense, against what is right and necessary in a democracy.

When a government is of, by and for the people, when an educated citizenry (in Thomas Jefferson's words) is essential to a democracy, it is imperative that we all know what the government does in our name. How else can we determine how to vote, who to support or what to oppose? Whistleblowers play a crucial role in this process. When the government willfully seeks to conceal its actions, someone is required to step up and act with courage and selflessness.

That our current government has been willing to fight for more than seven years—maybe all the way to the Supreme Court—to weaken legal whistleblowing protections tells a tale of our times. That it seeks to silence whistleblowers at a moment when their disclosures are just beginning to reveal the scope of our unconstitutional national security state is cause for great concern. That the government demands whistleblowers work within the system and then seeks to modify that same system to thwart them goes beyond hypocrisy.

This is the very definition of post-constitutional America where legality and il-legality blur—and always in the government's favor; where the founding principles of our nation only apply when, as, and if the executive sees fit. The devil is indeed in the details.

Air Marshal Whistleblower Wins 7–2 Supreme Court Victory

Government Accountability Project, January 21, 2015

Today, after an 8 $\frac{1}{2}$ year legal ordeal, federal air marshal whistleblower and GAP client Robert MacLean won a Supreme Court decision affirming that his disclosures were covered by the Whistleblower Protection Act (WPA). MacLean publicly warned in 2003 that the Department of Homeland Security (DHS) planned to pull federal air marshals, sworn to protect the public, from commercial aircrafts targeted for an ambitious overseas terrorist attack. The key legal issue was whether the law's statutory free speech rights can be canceled by agency secrecy regulations.

GAP Legal Director Tom Devine, MacLean's attorney since 2010, commented:

> In the Supreme Court's first case testing the Whistleblower Protection Act, freedom of speech won with an exclamation point. Federal air marshal whistleblower Robert MacLean's 7-2 victory means that, after defending his rights for more than eight years, he will have a chance to achieve justice. The only issue left is whether MacLean was reasonable to believe that the government's decision to remove air marshals from targeted flights endangered the public, since the Department of Homeland Security had planned to go AWOL in the face of a more ambitious rerun of 9/11. The ruling is a historic victory for the right of individuals to make a difference through freedom of speech.

MacLean also responded to the Court's decision. He stated:

> I'm extremely honored and grateful that the Court decided on this case. Many great people from non-government organizations, the U.S. Office of Special Counsel, Congress, and the courts came together to make this happen. I believe this ruling will give other federal employees more confidence in exposing wrongdoing without breaking the law. No matter what happens, it will always be difficult for a person to risk his career when speaking out.

Background

In late July 2003, air marshal Robert MacLean received an unrestricted text message order. The Transportation Security Administration (TSA) was eliminating coverage of long-distance flights requiring overnight hotel stays. It was a stunning development, since all air marshals in the country had just completed emergency training to stop al Qaeda plans confirmed by U.S. and foreign intelligence for a more ambitious rerun of the 9/11 attack: this time long-distance flights to multiple U.S. cities and European capitals were targeted.

MacLean protested to his supervisor, and then an investigator within the DHS Office of Inspector General. Both agreed but said there was nothing he could do and should stay quiet. MacLean would not give up and he reached Congress through the media as a confidential source. Numerous senators immediately called press conferences to express outrage and threatened hearings about abandoning the public during an enemy attack. Within 24 hours, the agency reversed itself and reinstated protection, saying the order was a "mistake." Air marshal coverage was restored, and the hijacking was prevented.

Three years later, the agency identified MacLean as the whistleblower, and fired him for endangering the nation by violating agency secrecy regulations, after it retroactively labeled the text message as "Sensitive Security Information" on grounds that its release was "detrimental to aviation security." GAP represented MacLean first at the Merit Systems Protection Board, where he lost, and then the U.S. Court of Appeals for the Federal Circuit, where he prevailed unanimously twice. The court upheld the supremacy of statutory free speech rights over agency secrecy rules, and ruled even statutory bans on public disclosures must be specific so employees have clear notice. Undaunted, the Department of Justice continued its war on whistleblowers by appealing to the Supreme Court, which accepted the case.

The Hogan and Lovell law firm's Neal Katyal and a team of highly skilled lawyers joined with GAP in defending MacLean. Katyal was President Obama's former acting Solicitor General. Before the current victory, he had argued 21 Supreme Court cases (16 at the Department of Justice) and won them all. MacLean also received impressive solidarity through friend-of-the-court briefs from Congress, the Office of Special Counsel, national security professionals, airline consumer groups, a federal union, and good government organizations. None were filed supporting the government.

The Decision

Chief Justice John Roberts wrote the 7–2 majority opinion, which was based on two key issues to interpret the WPA's relevant limits. 5 USC 2302(b)(8)(A) does not protect public disclosures that are "specifically prohibited by law." The government argued that Department of Homeland Security (DHS) secrecy regulations qualified as prohibitions by "law" that override free speech rights passed by Congress.

The majority ruling unequivocally rejected that claim, which would have made agency compliance voluntary for statutory free speech rights: "[T]he question here is whether a disclosure specifically prohibited by regulation also is specifically prohibited by *law* under section 2302(b)(8)(A). The answer is no" (emphasis in decision). The Court explained that Congress used the term "law, rule or regulation" nine times in section 2302 and only used the word "law" one time, indicating they did not mean the same thing. The Court emphasized that the contrasting language was even used in the same sentence that the government relied on when seeking to cancel MacLean's rights.

The government also argued that these particular regulations should qualify as law, because Congress required DHS to issue appropriate secrecy rules. But the Court noted, "Outside of this case, however, the government was unable to find a single example of the word 'law' being used in this way. Not a single dictionary definition, not a single statute, not a single case."

The Court agreed that the government's translation would defeat the Whistleblower Protection Act's purpose.

The government's second major argument was that the Aviation Transportation Security Act (ATSA) itself was a specific statutory prohibition, because it ordered agency regulations to bar disclosures that the Transportation Security Administration chief believed would be "detrimental to the security of transportation." The Court's majority said the ATSA did not prohibit anything itself by ordering DHS to act. The impact is that Congress cannot relinquish its responsibility by delegating to agencies if it wants to cancel Whistleblower Protection Act free speech rights.

While agreeing that regulations cannot be statutory prohibitions, Justice Sonia Sotomayor joined by Justice Anthony Kennedy dissented on grounds that the ATSA is a statutory prohibition. Neither the majority nor the dissent commented on the basis of MacLean's victories at the Federal Circuit Court of Appeals. Those rulings held that the phrase "detrimental to the security of transportation" is not sufficiently specific for clear notice to government employees whether they can blow the whistle publicly. As a result, the Federal Circuit's ruling on that key issue remains the law of the land.

Devine concluded:

> The survival of the Whistleblower Protection Act was at stake in this case. After today's victory, freedom of speech is alive, well and stronger than ever.

VA Destroyed Records, Punished Whistleblower in Patient Death, Complaint Alleges

By Jim McElhatton
The Washington Times, January 15, 2015

Staff at the VA's Cleveland medical center destroyed records into the death of a patient to avoid unwanted publicity, then punished a whistleblower and put her under surveillance after she revealed lapses in the patient's care, the woman charged in a recent complaint.

Patricia Leligdon said superiors began retaliating against her in 2010 after she reported that VA medical staff could have done more to prevent the death of a veteran who died after an "altercation" with another veteran at a VA outpatient mental health clinic, according to a federal whistleblower lawsuit she recently filed against the Department of Veterans Affairs.

The accusations come as the VA tries to assure its own employees and Congress that whistleblowers won't be retaliated against for reporting on patient safety and management problems.

The VA's previous secretary, Eric K. Shinseki, was ousted last year after a scandal into the falsification of wait time data, which surfaced because of complaints from whistleblowers.

Ms. Leligdon, whose attorney could not be immediately reached for comment, says in her complaint that the retaliation occurred before and after the VA's change in leadership. And the complaint says she wasn't the only employee at the VA's Cleveland Medical Center subject to retaliation for voicing concerns about the workplace, according to the complaint.

"This cultural attribute is part of a broader culture of suppressing criticism by engaging in reprisals against those who engage in criticism or otherwise associated with such critics," the complaint states.

VA officials declined to comment on the accusations or the extent to which the agency utilizes surveillance to monitor its own employees in and out of the workplace.

"The case is being handled by the US Attorney's office and is ongoing so I am unable to comment," VA spokeswoman Ashley Trimble wrote in an email.

Ms. Leligdon, who supervised a staff of about a dozen social workers, said she was told not to go public with her belief that the VA could have done more for the patient in 2010, according to her complaint.

She also said that during a February 2011 VA ethics panel meeting, which she attended through a conference call, an unnamed caller referred to information that another employee was going to disclose through social media sites that "would have destroyed" the Cleveland VA medical center's reputation.

According to Ms. Leligdon, the caller said a VA privacy official destroyed the evidence the other person would have disclosed, and the privacy official later issued a memo cautioning employees about a prohibition against sharing information about "personal activities occurring within the medical center" on social media.

The name of the veteran who died is not disclosed in the complaint, but the lawsuit says Ms. Leligdon and other VA personnel received subpoenas to testify in a hearing that never took place because the case was settled.

She said she was passed over for promotions, blackballed by staff and subject to increasing surveillance, and she sent letters to Mr. Shinseki, Attorney General Eric H. Holder Jr. and Ohio Attorney General Mike DeWine about the "coverup of unlawful activity," evidence destruction and the ongoing surveillance.

In March 2014 the VA medical center "stepped up its attacks" by issuing one disciplinary action after another and "escalating its unlawful surveillance" of Ms. Leligdon, she said in her complaint.

She said the retaliation continued even after the ouster of Mr. Shinseki and a June 13 memo by then–Acting VA Secretary Sloan Gibson hailing the VA's "unwavering" commitment to employee protections under the federal whistleblower statute.

Earlier this month, Rep. Jeff Miller, Florida Republican and chairman of the House Committee on Veterans' Affairs, told new VA Secretary Robert McDonald that his committee was investigating the agency's treatment of whistleblowers.

He also called on the agency to turn over disciplinary records in the case of a VA credentialing official in Puerto Rico who says he was suspended after notifying the VA about the late-night drug arrest of a high-ranking official, who was ultimately cleared of the charges.

Former CIA Officer Jeffrey Sterling Convicted in Leak Case

By Matt Zapotosky
The Washington Post, January 26, 2015

A former CIA officer who was involved in a highly secretive operation to give faulty nuclear plans to Iran was convicted Monday of providing classified information about his work to a *New York Times* reporter—a significant win for federal prosecutors and a presidential administration that has worked zealously to root out leakers.

As guilty verdicts were read on all nine criminal counts, Jeffrey Sterling stared emotionless at the jurors who decided his fate. His wife, seated in the courtroom behind him, sobbed.

The 47-year-old Missouri man is scheduled to be sentenced April 24 and remains free until then.

In a statement, Attorney General Eric H. Holder Jr. said the verdict was a "just and appropriate outcome."

"The disclosures placed lives at risk," Holder said. "And they constituted an egregious breach of the public trust by someone who had sworn to uphold it."

Sterling was accused of a breach that ultimately closed off one of the few avenues the United States had to stem the development of Iran's nuclear program.

But the prosecution also was notable because it spawned a First Amendment confrontation between a Pulitzer Prize–winning reporter and the Justice Department. And it might be one of the greatest courtroom successes of a presidential administration that has pursued more leak cases than all of its predecessors combined.

Jurors in the U.S. District Court in Alexandria deliberated for one whole day and sizable parts of two others before reaching their verdict. Earlier Monday, they told the judge in a note that they could not come to an agreement on several counts.

Other leak cases have resulted in pleas, at least one with terms favorable to the defendant. Former National Security Agency manager and accused leaker Thomas A. Drake pleaded to a reduced charge that called for no prison time. Prosecutors reached an agreement that brought a harsher penalty for former CIA officer John Kiriakou, who was sentenced to 2½ years in prison for disclosing a covert operative's name to a reporter.

Federal authorities are still considering charges against several high-profile individuals in other probes, including former CIA director David H. Petraeus, veteran

State Department diplomat Robin Raphel and retired Marine Gen. James E. "Hoss" Cartwright.

Dan French, a former U.S. attorney for the Northern District of New York who now does white-collar work at Hiscock & Barclay, said no matter whether prosecutors had won or lost the Sterling case, they are likely to aggressively prosecute leaks they deem serious in the future.

"I just think they're going to bring these cases continuously to demonstrate that type of conduct by a government employee or a government contractor is going to be prosecuted, because the risk is just too grave," he said.

Sterling, who faced charges under the Espionage Act, was first accused in 2010 of giving classified information to *New York Times* reporter and author James Risen for his 2006 book, *State of War*. Prosecutors alleged—and jurors apparently agreed—that Sterling was trying to get revenge on the CIA when he talked to Risen about an operation meant to deter Iran's nuclear program.

Sterling, who was fired in the early 2000s, had sued the agency over alleged discrimination and also sparred with officials about publishing a memoir describing some of his work.

The case drew special attention when federal prosecutors initially sought to subpoena Risen to testify against his will. Though they won in court, the Justice Department ultimately decided not to put the reporter on the stand at the trial. Risen had vowed to go to jail before he would reveal any sources.

Through his attorney, Risen declined to comment for this article. Holder said in his statement that the verdict proved "it is possible to fully prosecute unauthorized disclosures that inflict harm upon our national security without interfering with journalists' ability to do their jobs." Since his department's legal battles with Risen, Holder has tightened the guidelines governing investigations that involve journalists.

The trial itself was something of a spectacle, with CIA officers testifying behind a retractable gray screen as they described suitcases full of cash, clandestine meetings and fictitious back stories. The case against Sterling was largely circumstantial—there were no recorded phone conversations or captured e-mail exchanges that show that he leaked classified information to Risen—and that required prosecutors' to delve deeply into Sterling's work and the details of Risen's book.

By prosecutors' account, Sterling was the only potential source who had a relationship with Risen, knew all of the information from the chapter at issue and had a motive to discuss his clandestine work. They argued that the book—which suggested that the secret operation might actually have helped further Iran's nuclear research—was somewhat inaccurate and that it cast Sterling as a hero and the CIA as hapless.

"Jeffrey Sterling's spin is what appears in the book," prosecutor Eric Olshan said.

Defense attorneys posited several people other than Sterling who could have served as Risen's sources, and they suggested Sterling was unlikely to have given the reporter any information. They argued that some information in the book could not have come from Sterling, because it addressed things that happened after he left the CIA or contained details that he would not have known or remembered.

Sterling defense attorney Barry Pollack said after the hearing that attorneys plan to take the case to a higher court.

"This is a sad day for Mr. Sterling and his wife," Pollack said. "We will pursue all legal avenues with the trial court and on appeal to challenge Mr. Sterling's conviction."

Double Standard for Leaking Endangers the Nation

By Linda Lewis
Whistleblowing Today, January 21, 2015

Reportedly, investigators have recommended indictment of disgraced former Central Intelligence Agency Director David Petraeus on charges of leaking classified information.

> Investigators concluded that, whether or not the disclosure harmed national security, it amounted to a significant security breach in the office of one of the nation's most trusted intelligence leaders. They recommended that Mr. Petraeus face charges, saying lower-ranking officials had been prosecuted for far less. (*New York Times*, Jan. 9)

Attorney General Eric Holder says the decision is likely to be made "at the highest levels" of the Justice Department. But Petraeus, who is accused of sharing classified information with a biographer/mistress, is unlikely to ever see a prison cell. Influential Washington insiders immediately began lobbying the administration to grant a crony immunity.

Members of the Senate intelligence committee had high praise for the man who shielded government officials from accountability for drone assassinations and torture. "One of America's finest military leaders," wrote Senators John McCain and Lindsay Graham. "A very brilliant man," gushed Senator Diane Feinstein.

Sounding like the Dowager Countess of Grantham, Feinstein expressed shock that someone would even consider subjecting a person of Petraeus' high status to prosecution.

> This man has suffered enough, in my view. He's the four-star general of our generation. I saw him in Iraq. He put together the Army Field Manual. He put together the Awakening and how it worked out. He, I think, is a very brilliant man. – Feinstein (CNN) [Excerpt from transcript by Democracy Now!]

Changing course, Feinstein portrayed Petraeus as Everyman, deserving of sympathy from the masses (who likely would never get the special treatment requested for Petraeus).

> People aren't perfect. He made a mistake. He lost his job as CIA director because of it. I mean, how much do you want to punish somebody? (CNSNews)

If Americans are not filling the streets with cries of *Je suis Petraeus!,* possibly it's because they fear being shot down or tear-gassed by police in armored vehicles. Perhaps they see the hypocrisy in Feinstein demanding relentless prosecution of the "little guy," whether he is smoking pot or disclosing government abuses. They may recall Feinstein telling them to forget about clemency for Edward Snowden, and Obama condemning Bradley (now Chelsea) Manning.

Yes, we are all one except for the many occasions when we are not. The Petraeus case shines a light on Washington's double standard that immunizes people in positions of power and their loyal cronies, but demands harsh punishment for others.

> Long-standing mavens of DC political power literally believe that they and their class-comrades are too noble, important and elevated to be subjected to the rule of law to which they subject everyone else. They barely even disguise it any more. It's the dynamic by which the Obama administration prosecuted leakers with unprecedented aggression who disclose information that embarrasses them politically while ignoring or even sanctioning the leaks of classified information which politically glorify them. –Glenn Greenwald, *The Intercept*

The average American, who earns $35,293 a year, would be hard-pressed to understand how General Petraeus is "suffering." Since resigning in 2012, he has retained his security clearance (unlike the "other woman" in the scandal and numerous whistleblowers) and he continues to advise the White House. He has a top-tier attorney to handle his legal problems. He has multiple streams of income, including an Army pension ($220,000 a year), and teaching positions at the University of Southern California, the City University of New York (that involved Petraeus in a new scandal) and Harvard University. Mike Lofgren (BillMoyers.com) comments, "The Ivy League is, of course, the preferred bleaching tub and charm school of the American oligarchy."

Petraeus also gives speeches and, best of all, he is Chairman of the KKR Global Institute, a presumably very lucrative position created for him in 2013 by the private equity firm Kohlberg Kravis Roberts. KKR has been cagey as to the exact nature of Petraeus' expected contributions to the firm, and onlookers express puzzlement about his qualifications for the job. It seems fair to suppose that his CIA and Army expertise offer some potential benefit to the firm, whose investors include high net worth individuals and sovereign wealth funds (SWFs).

Experts have warned for several years about changes in the way SWFs invest that increase the potential for foreign governments to use them to undermine the economy and security of other countries, including the United States. Thomas Hemphill pointed out some of the risks in an article for *Thunderbird International Business Review.*

> Lyons (2007) and Luft (2008) argue that this form of "state capitalism" can be used to secure sensitive strategic assets in the infrastructure industries (e.g., telecommunications, media, energy, seaports, and financial services) and, in lieu of a direct military attack, undertake decisions contrary to the safety and security of the United States or other Western countries.

Researcher Alan Tonelson, in *American Economic Alert*, described another looming threat. "Foreign government investments from Persian Gulf oil kingdoms in particular . . . raise the somewhat different yet equally worrisome possibility of transfers to third parties, such as terrorist organizations or to rogue states like Iran and North Korea." But an investment corporation's chief responsibility is to maximize the returns of investors, including SWFs, and, Tonelson notes, government regulation has not caught up with developments in the investment industry.

For high-level leakers, it seems the safety net is always out. BoingBoing notes, "[C]urrent CIA director John Brennan, former CIA director Leon Panetta, and former CIA general counsel John Rizzo are just three of many high-ranking government officials who have gotten off with little to no punishment despite the fact we know they've leaked information to the media that the government considers classified." But, for whistleblowers, there is no safety net; only a steady stream of abuses.

National security whistleblowers have been fired, stripped of their security clearances, blacklisted from employment, imprisoned, held at gunpoint while their homes were ransacked, placed on the government's No Fly list, shunned, prosecuted under the Espionage Act, subjected to surveillance, maligned in national media, subjected to retaliatory mental examinations, stripped naked and held in solitary confinement while awaiting trial and declared guilty in advance by the Commander in Chief.

The government wants nothing less than complete destruction of the whistleblower—politically, socially, physically, financially and psychologically—to discourage others from whistleblowing. Calling this "reprisal" is too kind. It's bureaucratic terrorism designed to protect the organization from external accountability for waste, fraud and abuse. For examples, see the cases of Thomas Drake, Chelsea/Bradley Manning and John Kiriakou.

Retaliation occurs whether or not whistleblowers disclose classified information to the public, whether or not they go through authorized channels, whether or not their disclosure harms anyone. These are null factors, irrelevant to whether a whistleblower experiences retaliation; but they dominate the public debate as a purposeful distraction from a fundamental truth: The system abhors external accountability, a linchpin of our republic. Often, it has much to hide.

The officials who proposed leniency for Petraeus did so, apparently, without knowing details of the FBI's evidence against him. That is standard treatment for privileged leakers, for whom there is a presumption of innocence. In contrast, whistleblowers are presumed guilty of the most vile offenses and deserving of the most extreme punishment.

"Congressman Mike Rogers called for execution of Bradley/Chelsea Manning if found guilty."

"Sen. Feinstein denied that Edward Snowden is a whistle blower and said he was guilty of 'treason.'"

"Bill Nelson, formerly a member of the Senate Intelligence Committee, called Snowden's disclosures an 'act of treason'."

"Former CIA director James Woolsey told Fox News that Edward Snowden, who exposed illegal domestic spying, "should be prosecuted for treason" and 'hanged by his neck until he is dead'."

Sidebar: Even Aldrich Ames and Robert Hansen, two of America's most notorious spies, did not receive the death penalty.

Some of these extremely biased and hostile statements about whistleblowers were made by officials who are or were "official channels" for the receipt of whistleblower disclosures, and responsible for enforcement or oversight of whistleblower protections. *This is a huge red flag for potential whistleblowers in national security programs.*

One can argue that the Snowden and Manning cases are significantly different from cases like Petraeus' and Panetta's. But even when serious, documented harm resulted from leaks that were clear cases of espionage, culpable non-whistleblowers received a slap on the wrist. That was demonstrated in the case of Aldrich Ames, the notorious CIA mole, whose leaks to the Soviets had a devastating impact on US intelligence.

> The information he gave the Soviets led to the virtual annihilation of the agency's Soviet network. At least 10 CIA agents were executed. Others wound up in prison camps or had to flee to the West. Ames also compromised dozens of other operations, including vital communications intercepts. (Businessweek)

Ames escaped detection for nearly a decade due to the CIA's "boozy old-boys' club" culture, "overly concerned with protecting perks and deflecting scrutiny."

> Pegged by his bosses as a boozer who used CIA safe houses for sex, Ames nonetheless was promoted to a highly sensitive counterintelligence post in 1984. The FBI observed him meeting secretly with a Russian contact in 1986, but the CIA ignored the warning. He was transferred instead to Rome, where he was so drunk that the Italian police once fished him out of a gutter. Though he was ranked 197 out of 200 case officers in his division, Ames was put on a promotion panel to pass judgment on his colleagues (he also likely passed along their identities to the Soviets). In 1990, a female case officer alerted her bosses that Ames seemed suspiciously flush with cash . . . Yet he had received not a single reprimand in his 32-year career. The excuse? His superiors thought he was a "good briefer." (*Newsweek*)

Ultimately, an investigative report by the CIA's inspector general identified 23 current and former CIA employees that it said should be held accountable for the leaks. The job of deciding their fate fell to then CIA Director James "Hang 'em high" Woolsey. It's tempting to suppose that the man who wants to string up an NSA whistleblower came down hard on Ames' enablers. Instead, "Woolsey chose to issue letters of reprimand to 11 employees—seven of whom were retired—but no one was fired, demoted, suspended or reassigned."

Protecting and promoting incompetents is not unique to the CIA. In the military, the practice is known as "pass the trash." But judging from the details that emerged last week in the case of Aldrich Ames, the now infamous Soviet mole, the CIA's clubby Operations Directorate acted more like a mutual protection association than a spy agency

Subsequently, the Robert Hansen spying scandal erupted at the Federal Bureau of Investigation, an agency that "hates the very idea of any outside control or oversight," and routinely retaliates against whistleblowers. More recently, fraud and cronyism prevented the National Security Agency from detecting the 9/11 plot. The agency's retaliation against whistleblowers who tried within "official channels" to correct the problems led to a bigger scandal that focused attention on the earlier one. Still more scandals, at the Secret Service, the Interior Department, and the U.S. Navy, show that the "mutual protection association" is still alive in Washington, protected by a double standard that endangers everyone by allowing negligence, incompetence, and fraud to undermine important government functions.

Strict justice requires the government to treat Petraeus as it has whistleblowers by prosecuting him under the Espionage Act. But prosecuting anyone under the Act who is not spying for a foreign nation is unjust. Furthermore, it gravely undermines the public interest in disclosures of government wrongdoing. The best solution would be for Congress to amend the Act to limit its scope to classic espionage, i.e., the kind of spying conducted by Ames and Hansen.

Dana Gold, Senior Fellow at the Government Accountability Project, writes, "No one wins under the current paradigm that vilifies whistleblowers: not businesses, not government, not the public, and certainly not the whistleblowers."

4
Security in a Democracy

©Gary Miller/FilmMagic/Getty Images

Edward Snowden speaks via satellite from an undisclosed location during the South By Southwest Interactive Festival at the Austin Convention Center on March 10, 2014, in Austin, Texas.

Seeing Both Sides

Whistleblowers and whistleblowing can engender the gamut of reactions. There are those who view whistleblowers as courageous to the point of self-sacrificing, often short-circuiting their professional and personal lives in the cause of a greater good. And there are those who see whistleblowers as dangerous malcontents, wreaking havoc on society with their reckless revelations. "The term 'whistleblower' has always been ambiguous; one person's whistleblower is another's grandstanding gadfly," Steve Coll accurately observed in *The New Yorker*.

It is not simply a question of prevailing public attitude. Amid the passionate debate are some very real questions with very real legal ramifications. When—if ever—is it permissible to leak state or industrial secrets for the common good? Does inexcusable damage occur at the hands of these self-appointed reformers? As the information age speeds up, the layers and complexity of whistleblowing will only increase. And so, of course, will the questions it raises.

"The case for prosecution of whistleblowers," Gabriel Schoenfeld writes, "rests upon the enormous damage such leaks can inflict"—damage that can stymie the US's ongoing battle against the forces of global terror.

Schoenfeld represents a huge, significant slice of American public and judicial opinion. "There are some lawyers, scholars, commentators, and administrators who remain troubled by public sentiment and legal practice and interpretation that they feel are overly sympathetic and encouraging of whistleblowing," observes Roberta Ann Johnson. She continues: "A few opponents of the [perceived] whistleblower-friendly trend have argued that there is only a narrowly defined area in which whistleblowing is completely justified. It is when employees are themselves asked to do something illegal."

The academic Rahul Sagar argues, in his book *Secrets and Leaks*, that since the revelations of Daniel Ellsberg and the Pentagon Papers over four decades ago, "there has been a sense, that, if all else fails, citizens and lawmakers can rely on 'insiders' to blow the whistle on what classified information ought to be made public. But this is a remarkable conceit," he asserts. "Why should we believe that the press will always act in the public interest, especially when its role as information broker is shrouded in secrecy, thus preventing the public from ascertaining the motives and the precise actions of reporters, editors, and publishers, not to mention their sources?"

And the opposition to whistleblowing is not just rooted in simple theory—there are also those who claim that some revelations could constitute very real dangers. "In an apparent expansion of the government's secrecy powers," the *New York Times* reported in 2014, "the top official in charge of the classification system has decided that it was legitimate for the Marines to classify photographs that showed American forces posing with corpses of Taliban fighters in Afghanistan." The "Marines' rationale for classifying the photographs [was] that their dissemination could encourage attacks against troops."

Nonsense, retorts Jesselyn Radack, emphatically refuting the viewpoints of Schoenfeld, Sagar, et al. "Secrecy," she writes, "is a cornerstone of autocratic rule and unaccountable political systems, not democracies." That harsh view of whistleblowers renders "anyone who tries to bring forth information that would allow the public to exercise its sovereign prerogative of democratic debate be damned, or better yet, sent to prison." And, of course, Radack also represents a significant sector of American public opinion.

Because whistleblowing often does not fall into easily slotted categories, its opponents and defenders can come from some unexpected quarters. Charles Grassley, veteran Iowa Republican senator and hardly a wide-eyed radical, has loomed large in the annals of defending whistleblowers. Among other examples of advocacy, Grassley "authored amendments to the False Claims Act that gave private citizens more power to report fraudulent activity by government contractors and to sue in the name of the government." (*Washington Post*, April 10, 2014) The no-nonsense Senator Grassley opined that "whistleblowers are often treated like skunks at a picnic. It takes guts to put your career on the line to expose waste and fraud, and whistleblowers need senators who will listen and advocate for them."

There can be some broad-based ethical considerations about whistleblowing—not to mention the enormous, often catastrophic personal cost. One can—and should—construct a mental blueprint to determine if any potential revelations can do some genuine, unintended damage. Judy Nadler and Miriam Schulman have compiled some guidelines. Whistleblowing should be undertaken only if normal channels have failed—if the official mechanisms to report wrongdoing cease to function. Then there is the analysis of what sort of information is being disclosed: the level of confidentiality the whistleblower is breaking. Another consideration is "whether the potential leaker has a specific obligation, legal or ethical, to protect the information, or has the information only because another person violated his or her obligation to keep it secret. If so, then it is a much more serious matter to reveal it."

The unfortunate constant is that "making secrets and managing them have always been a great source of political power, and the closer politicians get to this power, the more enamored of it they become." (Jack Shafer, *Foreign Affairs*) "'Where an excess of power prevails,' to steal a phrase from James Madison, almost no leader can resist going too far in accomplishing his goals if the opportunity presents itself. And if you are the president of the United States, opportunity knocks loudly several times a day."

In general, the attitude in official circles has not been favorable to whistleblowers. *Harper's* magazine has pointed out that "Although President Obama campaigned on calls to respect and protect whistleblowers, no sooner did he take office than the Justice Department adopted a diametrically opposite posture. Under [Attorney General] Eric Holder, the department fully embraced. . . the Espionage Act of 1917 to prosecute civil servants accused of leaking materials that it felt compromised national security." That act—almost a century old—has very real applications.

"[T]he Obama administration," Jane Mayer writes in *The New Yorker*, "has pursued leak prosecutions with a surprising relentlessness." Mayer quoted Yale law professor Jack Balkin, who "agrees that the increase in leak prosecutions is part of a large transformation. 'We are witnessing the bipartisan normalization and legitimization of a national-surveillance state,' he says." Since 9/11, the security apparatus in the United States has grown dramatically, with upwards of two million people holding confidential or top-secret clearances and a newly emergent, increasingly influential counterterrorism industry. President Obama has drawn "a sharp distinction between whistleblowers who exclusively reveal wrongdoing and those who jeopardize national security." These distinctions, of course, may not matter to the defenders of Edward Snowden, Chelsea Manning, and some of the other high-profile cases who have run into harsh legal retribution.

But to further muddy the waters, the White House, in 2012, "released a presidential directive extending legal protections to intelligence community employees who expose government fraud, waste, or abuse. Advocates for greater transparency and accountability in government applauded the move." (Elizabeth Goltein, *Huffington Post*)

There is also the contention—shared by many—that whistleblowing has deep roots in the American tradition of openness and democracy. Daniel Ellsberg, who leaked the massive Pentagon Papers in the early 1970s, "deferred graduate school at Harvard to remain on active duty in the Marine Corps," Chase Madar has written. "Ellsberg saw his high-risk exposure of the disastrous and deceitful nature of the Vietnam War as fully consonant with his long career of patriotic service in and out of uniform." Madar continues: "Transparency in statecraft was not invented last week by WikiLeaks creator Julian Assange. It is a longstanding American tradition."

One solution—or, at least a way out—is postulated by David Cay Johnston in *Newsweek*. "Why assume that leakers must risk all? Why assume leakers must be prosecuted?" he writes. "The U.S. should enact a public interest defense. Leakers could still face prosecution, but they could try to persuade a jury that their acts were justified in defense of the republic. After all, the government is not a power unto itself, but derives its consent from the people." Johnson's proposal notably takes no explicit side in the ongoing conflict, only recognizes that whistleblowing is basically here to stay—and offers some sort of workable solution.

A workable solution, though, is a tall order. Whistleblowing is such a contentious issue that even its very definition—what is whistleblowing, exactly?—remains a source of debate. And that debate extends into so many other spheres of law and public policy: the nature of dissent, the government's role in maintaining state security, the public's right to know. As long as there is perceived wrongdoing and the attendant secrets, there will be whistleblowers. And their defenders and detractors—in the courts, the government, and the media—will only grow more vociferous.

Bibliography

Coll, Steve. "The Spy Who Said Too Much." *The New Yorker*, April 1, 2013; http://www.newyorker.com/magazine/2013/04/01/the-spy-who-said-too-much

Galveston, W.W. "A Case for Clemency for Snowden." *The Economist*, January 10, 2014; http://www.economist.com/blogs/democracyinamerica/2014/01/whistle-blowers-and-national-security.

Goltein, Elizabeth. "A Mixed Message for National Security Whistleblowers." *Huffington Post*, December 22, 2012; http://www.huffingtonpost.com/elizabeth-goitein/obama-whistleblowers_b_1989629.html

Harris, Savaria, and Mitka Baker. "Lessons from the Year of the Whistleblower: A Changing Regulatory Regime." *Inside Counsel*, January 16, 2015; http://www.insidecounsel.com/2015/01/16/lessons-from-the-year-of-the-whistleblower-a-chang

Hicks, Josh. "Sen. Charles Grassley Plans New Whistleblower-Protection Caucus." *Washington Post*, April 10, 2014; http://www.washingtonpost.com/blogs/federal-eye/wp/2014/04/10/sen-charles-grassley-plans-new-whistleblower-protection-caucus/

Horton, Scott. "A Setback for Obama's War on Whistleblowers." *Harper's*, August 9, 2011; http://harpers.org/blog/2011/08/a-setback-in-obamas-war-on-whistle-blowers/

Johnson, Roberta Ann. *Whistleblowing: When It Works—and Why* (Boulder, CO: Lynne Rienner Publishers, 2003).

Johnston, David Cay. "Hounding Whistleblowers Is Wrong." *Newsweek*, October 28, 2013; http://www.newsweek.com/hounding-whistleblowers-wrong-1164

Lee, Timothy B. "Daniel Ellsberg: 'I'm sure that President Obama would have sought a life sentence in my case.'" *The Washington Post*, June 5, 2013; http://www.washingtonpost.com/blogs/wonkblog/wp/2013/06/05/daniel-ellsberg-im-sure-that-president-obama-would-have-sought-a-life-sentence-in-my-case/

Madar, Chase. "Alleged WikiLeaks Whistleblower Bradley Manning Is a Hero." In Berlatsky, Noah, ed., *Whistleblowers* (Farmington Hills, MI: Greenhaven Press, 2012).

Madar, Chase. "The Trials of Bradley Manning." *The Nation*, July 31, 2013; http://www.thenation.com/article/175512/trials-bradley-manning.

Mayer, Jane. "The Secret Sharer." *The New Yorker*, May 23, 2011; http://www.newyorker.com/magazine/2011/05/23/the-secret-sharer

Nadler, Judy, and Miriam Schulman. "Whistleblowing in the Public Sector." Markkula Center for Applied Ethics, Santa Clara University Web site; http://www.scu.edu/ethics/practicing/focusareas/government_ethics/introduction/whistleblowing.html

Radack, Jesselyn. "Whistleblowers Expose Illegal Activity, Not Government Secrets." In Berlatsky, Noah, ed., *Whistleblowers* (Farmington Hills, MI: Greenhaven Press, 2012).

Sagar, Rahul. *Secrets and Leaks: The Dilemma of State Secrecy* (Princeton, NJ: Princeton University Press, 2013).

Savage, Charlie. "Official Backs Marines' Move to Classify Photos of Forces with Taliban Bodies." *New York Times*, June 10, 2014; http://www.nytimes.com/2014/06/11/us/official-backs-marines-move-to-classify-photos-of-forces-with-taliban-bodies.html?_r=0

Schoenfeld, Gabriel. "Those Who Expose National Secrets Should be Punished." In Berlatsky, Noah, ed., *Whistleblowers* (Farmington Hills, MI: Greenhaven Press, 2012).

Shafer, Jack. "Live and Let Leak." *Foreign Affairs*, March/April 2014.

Shorrock, Tim. "Obama's Crackdown on Whistleblowers." *The Nation*, March 26, 2013; http://www.thenation.com/article/173521/obamas-crackdown-whistleblowers?page=0,0

Smith, Andrew. " 'There Were Hundreds of Us Crying out for Help': The Afterlife of the Whistleblower," *The Guardian*, November 22, 2014; http://www.theguardian.com/society/2014/nov/22/there-were-hundreds-of-us-crying-out-for-help-afterlife-of-whistleblower

Solomon, Norman and Marcy Wheeler. "The Government War Against Reporter James Risen." *The Nation*, October 8, 2014; http://www.thenation.com/article/181919/government-war-against-reporter-james-risen?page=0,3

Van Buren, Peter. "Edward Snowden's Long Flight Home." *The Huffington Post*, July 1, 2013; http://www.huffingtonpost.com/peter-van-buren/edward-snowden-flight_b_3528401.html

Wilentz, Sean. "Would You Feel Differently about Snowden, Greenwald, and Assange if You Knew What They Really Thought?" *The New Republic*, January 19, 2014; http://www.newrepublic.com/article/116253/edward-snowden-glenn-greenwald-julian-assange-what-they-believe

Kiriakou and Stuxnet:
The Danger of the Still-Escalating Obama Whistleblower War

By Glenn Greenwald
The Guardian, January 27, 2013

The only official punished for the illegal NSA program was the one who discussed it. The same is now true of torture.

The permanent US national security state has used extreme secrecy to shield its actions from democratic accountability ever since its creation after World War II. But those secrecy powers were dramatically escalated in the name of 9/11 and the War on Terror, such that most of what the US government now does of any significance is completely hidden from public knowledge. Two recent events—the sentencing last week of CIA torture whistleblower John Kirikaou to 30 months in prison and the invasive investigation to find the *New York Times'* source for its reporting on the US role in launching cyberwarfare at Iran—demonstrate how devoted the Obama administration is not only to maintaining, but increasing, these secrecy powers.

When WikiLeaks published hundreds of thousands of classified diplomatic cables in 2010, government defenders were quick to insist that most of those documents were banal and uninteresting. And that's true: most (though by no means all) of those cables contained nothing of significance. That, by itself, should have been a scandal. All of those documents were designated as "secret," making it a crime for government officials to reveal their contents—despite how insignificant most of it was. That revealed how the US government reflexively—really automatically—hides anything and everything it does behind this wall of secrecy: they have made it a felony to reveal even the most inconsequential and pedestrian information about its actions.

This is why whistleblowing—or, if you prefer, unauthorized leaks of classified information—has become so vital to preserving any residual amounts of transparency. Given how subservient the federal judiciary is to government secrecy claims, it is not hyperbole to describe unauthorized leaks as the only real avenue remaining for learning about what the US government does—particularly for discovering the bad acts it commits. *That* is why the Obama administration is waging an unprecedented war against it—a war that continually escalates—and it is why it is so threatening.

To understand the Obama White House's obsession with punishing leaks—as evidenced by its historically unprecedented war on whistleblowers—just consider how virtually every significant revelation of the bad acts of the US government over the last decade came from this process. Unauthorized leaks are how we learned about the Bush administration's use of torture, the NSA's illegal eavesdropping on Americans without the warrants required by the criminal law, the abuses at Abu Ghraib, the secret network of CIA "black sites" beyond the reach of law or human rights monitoring, the targeting by Obama of a US citizen for assassination without due process, the re-definition of "militant" to mean "any military age male in a strike zone," the video of a US Apache helicopter gunning down journalists and rescuers in Baghdad, the vastly under-counted civilians deaths caused by the war in Iraq, and the Obama administration's campaign to pressure Germany and Spain to cease criminal investigations of the US torture regime.

In light of this, it should not be difficult to understand why the Obama administration is so fixated on intimidating whistleblowers and going far beyond any prior administration - including those of the secrecy-obsessed Richard Nixon and George W. Bush—to plug all leaks. It's because those methods are the only ones preventing the US government from doing whatever it wants in complete secrecy and without any accountability of any kind.

Silencing government sources is the key to disabling investigative journalism and a free press. That is why the New Yorker's Jane Mayer told whistleblowing advocate Jesselyn Radack last April: *"when our sources are prosecuted, the news-gathering process is criminalized, so it's incumbent upon all journalists to speak up."*

Indeed, if you talk to leading investigative journalists they will tell you that the Obama war on whistleblowers has succeeded in intimidating not only journalists' sources but also investigative journalists themselves. Just look at the way the DOJ has pursued and threatened with prison one of the most accomplished and institutionally protected investigative journalists in the country—James Risen—and it's easy to see why the small amount of real journalism done in the US, most driven by unauthorized leaks, is being severely impeded. This morning's *Washington Post* article on the DOJ's email snooping to find the NYT's Stuxnet source included this anonymous quote: *"People are feeling less open to talking to reporters given this uptick. There is a definite chilling effect in government due to these investigations."*

For authoritarians who view assertions of government power as inherently valid and government claims as inherently true, none of this will be bothersome. Under that mentality, if the government decrees that something shall be secret, then it should be secret, and anyone who defies that dictate should be punished as a felon—or even a traitor. That view is typically accompanied by the belief that we can and should trust our leaders to be good and do good even if they exercise power in the dark, so that transparency is not only unnecessary but undesirable.

But the most basic precepts of human nature, political science, and the American founding teach that power exercised in the dark will be inevitably abused. Secrecy is the linchpin of the abuse of power. That's why those who wield political power are always driven to destroy methods of transparency. About this fact, Thomas Jefferson wrote in an 1804 letter to John Tyler [emphasis added]:

> "Our first object should therefore be, to leave open to him all the avenues of truth. The most effectual hitherto found, is freedom of the press. **It is therefore, the first shut up by those who fear the investigation of their actions.**"

About all that, Yale law professor David A. Schultz observed: "For Jefferson, a free press was the tool of public criticism. It held public officials accountable, opening them up to the judgment of people who could decide whether the government was doing good or whether it had anything to hide. . . . A democratic and free society is dependent upon the media to inform."

There should be no doubt that destroying this method of transparency—*not* protection of legitimate national security secrets—is the primary effect, and almost certainly the intent, of this unprecedented war on whistleblowers. Just consider the revelations that have prompted the Obama DOJ's war on whistleblowers, whereby those who leak are not merely being prosecuted, but threatened with decades or even life in prison for "espionage" or "aiding the enemy."

Does anyone believe it would be better if we remained ignorant about the massive waste, corruption and illegality plaguing the NSA's secret domestic eavesdropping program (Thomas Drake); or the dangerously inept CIA effort to infiltrate the Iranian nuclear program but which ended up assisting that program (Jeffrey Sterling); or the overlooking of torture squads in Iraq, the gunning down of journalists and rescuers in Baghdad, or the pressure campaign to stop torture investigations in Spain and Germany (Bradley Manning); or the decision by Obama to wage cyberwar on Iran, which the Pentagon itself considers an act of war (current DOJ investigation)?

Like all of the Obama leak prosecutions none of those revelations resulted in any tangible harm, yet all revealed vital information about what our government was doing in secret. As long-time DC lawyer Abbe Lowell, who represents indicted whistleblower Stephen Kim, put it: what makes the Obama DOJ's prosecutions historically unique is that they "don't distinguish between bad people—people who spy for other governments, people who sell secrets for money—and people who are accused of having conversations and discussions." Not only doesn't it draw this distinction, but it is focused almost entirely on those who leak in order to expose wrongdoing and bring about transparency and accountability.

That is the primary impact of all of this. A Bloomberg report last October on this intimidation campaign summarized the objections this way: *"the president's crackdown chills dissent, curtails a free press and betrays Obama's initial promise to 'usher in a new era of open government.'"*

The Obama administration does not dislike leaks of classified information. To the contrary, it is a prolific exploiter of exactly those types of leaks—when they can be used to propagandize the citizenry to glorify the president's image as a tough guy, advance his political goals or produce a multi-million-dollar Hollywood film about his greatest conquest. Leaks are only objectionable when they undercut that propaganda by exposing government deceit, corruption and illegality.

Few events have vividly illustrated this actual goal as much as the lengthy prison sentence this week meted out to former CIA officer John Kiriakou. It's true that Kiriakou is not a pure anti-torture hero given that, in his first public disclosures, he made inaccurate claims about the efficacy of waterboarding. But he did also unequivocally condemn waterboarding and other methods as torture. And, as FAIR put it this week, whatever else is true: *"The only person to do time for the CIA's torture policies appears to be a guy who spoke publicly about them, not any of the people who did the actual torturing."*

Despite zero evidence of any harm from his disclosures, the federal judge presiding over his case—the reliably government-subservient US District Judge Leonie Brinkema—said she "would have given Kiriakou much more time if she could." As usual, the only real criminals in the government are those who expose or condemn its wrongdoing.

Exactly the same happened with revelations by the *New York Times* of the illegal Bush NSA warrantless eavesdropping program. None of the officials who eavesdropped on Americans without the warrants required by law were prosecuted. The telecoms that illegally cooperated were retroactively immunized from all legal accountability by the US Congress. The only person to suffer recriminations from that scandal was Thomas Tamm, the mid-level DOJ official who discovered the program and told the *New York Times* about it, and then had his life ruined with vindictive investigations.

This Obama whistleblower war has nothing to do with national security. It has nothing to do with punishing those who harm the country with espionage or treason.

It has everything to do with destroying those who expose high-level government wrongdoing. It is particularly devoted to preserving the government's ability to abuse its power in secret by intimidating and deterring future acts of whistleblowing and impeding investigative journalism. This Obama whistleblower war continues to escalate because it triggers no objections from Republicans (who always adore government secrecy) or Democrats (who always adore what Obama does), but most of all because it triggers so few objections from media outlets, which—at least in theory—suffer the most from what is being done.

UPDATE

Kevin Gosztola of Firedoglake this week interviewed Kiriakou and provides much more detail on the charges against him, including the overblown allegation that he leaked the name of one of the torturers to a journalist who then passed it on to the ACLU for filing in a classified court pleading. It's well worth reading the background of what was done to Kiriakou, who—whatever else you may think of his actions—was, as Gosztola writes, "the first member of the agency to publicly acknowledge that torture was official US policy under the administration of President George W. Bush."

Meanwhile, Trevor Timm of Electronic Frontier Foundation and the Freedom of the Press Foundation (of which I'm a Board Member) has more on the highly invasive and inappropriate tactics being used by the DOJ to try to root out the NYT's Stuxnet source.

UPDATE II

Speaking of the Obama administration's propensity to leak classified information for propagandistic and other political purposes, numerous senators have indicated their intent to investigate whether the CIA and other officials passed classified information about the bin Laden raid to the makers of *Zero Dark Thirty* in order to influence the film. If you have any doubts about whether this happened, just consider what *ZDT* screenwriter Mark Boal just said in *Time* Magazine about this film and decide for yourself.

On Whistleblowers and Government Threats of Investigation

By Glenn Greenwald
The Guardian, June 7, 2013

We followed Wednesday's story about the NSA's bulk telephone record-gathering with one yesterday about the agency's direct access to the servers of the world's largest internet companies. I don't have time at the moment to address all of the fallout because—to borrow someone else's phrase—I'm Looking Forward to future revelations that are coming (and coming shortly), not Looking Backward to ones that have already come.

But I do want to make two points. One is about whistleblowers, and the other is about threats of investigations emanating from Washington:

1) Ever since the Nixon administration broke into the office of Daniel Ellsberg's psychoanalyst's office, the tactic of the US government has been to attack and demonize whistleblowers as a means of distracting attention from their own exposed wrongdoing and destroying the credibility of the messenger so that everyone tunes out the message. That attempt will undoubtedly be made here.

I'll say more about all that shortly, but for now: as these whistleblowing acts becoming increasingly demonized ("reprehensible", declared Director of National Intelligence James Clapper yesterday), please just spend a moment considering the options available to someone with access to numerous Top Secret documents.

They could easily enrich themselves by selling those documents for huge sums of money to foreign intelligence services. They could seek to harm the US government by acting at the direction of a foreign adversary and covertly pass those secrets to them. They could gratuitously expose the identity of covert agents.

None of the whistleblowers persecuted by the Obama administration as part of its unprecedented attack on whistleblowers has done any of that: not one of them. Nor have those who are responsible for these current disclosures.

They did not act with any self-interest in mind. The opposite is true: they undertook great personal risk and sacrifice for one overarching reason: to make their fellow citizens aware of what their government is doing in the dark. Their objective is to educate, to democratize, to create accountability for those in power.

The people who do this are heroes. They are the embodiment of heroism. They do it knowing exactly what is likely to be done to them by the planet's most powerful government, but they do it regardless. They don't benefit in any way from these acts. I don't want to over-simplify: human beings are complex, and usually act with multiple, mixed motives. But read this outstanding essay[1] on this week's disclosures from *The Atlantic*'s security expert, Bruce Schneier, to understand why these brave acts are so crucial.

Those who step forward to blow these whistles rarely benefit at all. The ones who benefit are you. You discover what you should know but what is hidden from you: namely, the most consequential acts being taken by those with the greatest power, and how those actions are affecting your life, your country and your world.

In 2008, candidate Obama decreed that "often the best source of information about waste, fraud, and abuse in government is an existing government employee committed to public integrity and willing to speak out," and he hailed whistleblowing as:

> "acts of courage and patriotism, which can sometimes save lives and often save taxpayer dollars, [and] should be encouraged rather than stifled as they have been during the Bush administration."

The current incarnation of Obama prosecutes those same whistlelblowers at double the number of all previous presidents combined, and spent the campaign season boasting about it.

The 2008 version of Obama was right. As the various attacks are inevitably unleashed on the whistleblower(s) here, they deserve the gratitude and—especially—the support of everyone, including media outlets, for the noble acts that they have undertaken for the good of all of us. When it comes to what the Surveillance State is building and doing in the dark, we are much more informed today than we were yesterday, and will be much more informed tomorrow than we are today, thanks to them.

(2) Like puppets reading from a script, various Washington officials almost immediately began spouting all sorts of threats about "investigations" they intend to launch about these disclosures. This has been their playbook for several years now: they want to deter and intimidate anyone and everyone who might shed light on what they're doing with their abusive, manipulative exploitation of the power of law to punish those who bring about transparency.

That isn't going to work. It's beginning completely to backfire on them. It's precisely because such behavior reveals their true character, their propensity to abuse power, that more and more people are determined to bring about accountability and transparency for what they do.

They can threaten to investigate all they want. But as this week makes clear, and will continue to make clear, the ones who will actually be investigated are them.

The way things are supposed to work is that we're supposed to know virtually everything about what they do: that's why they're called *public* servants. They're supposed to know virtually nothing about what we do: that's why we're called *private* individuals.

This dynamic—the hallmark of a healthy and free society—has been radically reversed. Now, they know everything about what we do, and are constantly building systems to know more. Meanwhile, we know less and less about what they do, as they build walls of secrecy behind which they function. That's the imbalance that needs to come to an end. No democracy can be healthy and functional if the most consequential acts of those who wield political power are completely unknown to those to whom they are supposed to be accountable.

There seems to be this mentality in Washington that as soon as they stamp TOP SECRET on something they've done we're all supposed to quiver and allow them to do whatever they want without transparency or accountability under its banner. These endless investigations and prosecutions and threats are designed to bolster that fear-driven dynamic. But it isn't working. It's doing the opposite.

The times in American history when political power was constrained was when they went too far and the system backlashed and imposed limits. That's what happened in the mid-1970s when the excesses of J. Edgar Hoover and Richard Nixon became so extreme that the legitimacy of the political system depended upon it imposing restraints on itself. And that's what is happening now as the government continues on its orgies of whistleblower prosecutions, trying to criminalize journalism, and building a massive surveillance apparatus that destroys privacy, all in the dark. The more they overreact to measures of accountability and transparency—the more they so flagrantly abuse their power of secrecy and investigations and prosecutions—the more quickly that backlash will arrive.

I'm going to go ahead and take the Constitution at its word that we're guaranteed the right of a free press. So, obviously, are other people doing so. And that means that it isn't the people who are being threatened who deserve and will get the investigations, but those issuing the threats who will get that. That's why there's a free press. That's what *adversarial* journalism means.

Note

1.   http://www.theatlantic.com/politics/archive/2013/06/what-we-dont-know-about-spying-on-citizens-scarier-than-what-we-know/276607/

Demonizing Edward Snowden: Which Side Are You On?

By John Cassidy
The New Yorker, June 24, 2013

As I write this, a bunch of reporters are flying from Moscow to Havana on an Aeroflot Airbus 330, but Edward Snowden isn't sitting among them. His whereabouts are unknown. He might still be in the V.I.P. lounge at Sheremetyevo International Airport. He could have left on another plane. There are even suggestions that he has taken shelter in the Ecuadorian Embassy in Moscow.

What we do know is that, on this side of the Atlantic, efforts are being stepped up to demonize Snowden, and to delegitimize his claim to be a conscientious objector to the huge electronic-spying apparatus operated by the United States and the United Kingdom. "This is an individual who is not acting, in my opinion, with noble intent," General Keith Alexander, the head of the National Security Agency, told ABC's "This Week" on Sunday. "What Snowden has revealed has caused irreversible and significant damage to our country and to our allies." Over on CBS's "Face the Nation," Senator Dianne Feinstein, head of the Senate Intelligence Committee, said, "I don't think this man is a whistle-blower... he could have stayed and faced the music. I don't think running is a noble thought."

An unnamed senior Administration official joined the Snowden-bashing chorus, telling reporters, "Mr. Snowden's claim that he is focussed on supporting transparency, freedom of the press, and protection of individual rights and democracy is belied by the protectors he has potentially chosen: China, Russia, Cuba, Venezuela, and Ecuador. His failure to criticize these regimes suggests that his true motive throughout has been to injure the national security of the U.S., not to advance Internet freedom and free speech."

It is easy to understand, though not to approve of, why Administration officials, who have been embarrassed by Snowden's revelations, would seek to question his motives and exaggerate the damage he has done to national security. Feinstein, too, has been placed in a tricky spot. Tasked with overseeing the spooks and their spying operations, she appears to have done little more than nod.

More unnerving is the way in which various members of the media have failed to challenge the official line. Nobody should be surprised to see the *New York Post* running the headline: "Rogues' Gallery: Snowden Joins Long List of Notorious, Gutless Traitors Fleeing to Russia." But where are Snowden's defenders? As of Monday, the editorial pages of the *Times* and the *Washington Post*, the two most influential papers in the country, hadn't even addressed the Obama Administration's decision to charge Snowden with two counts of violating the Espionage Act and one count of theft.

If convicted on all three counts, the former N.S.A. contract-systems administrator could face thirty years in jail. On the Sunday-morning talk shows I watched, there weren't many voices saying that would be an excessive punishment for someone who has performed an invaluable public service. And the person who did aggressively defend Snowden's actions, Glenn Greenwald, the *Guardian* blogger who was one of the reporters to break the story, found himself under attack. After suggesting that Greenwald had "aided and abetted" Snowden, David Gregory, the host of NBC's *Meet the Press*, asked, "Why shouldn't you, Mr. Greenwald, be charged with a crime?"

After being criticized on Twitter, Gregory said that he wasn't taking a position on Snowden's actions—he was merely asking a question. I'm all for journalists asking awkward questions, too. But why aren't more of them being directed at Hayden and Feinstein and Obama, who are clearly intent on attacking the messenger?

To get a different perspective on Snowden and his disclosures, here's a portion of an interview that ABC—the Australian Broadcasting Company, not the Disney subsidiary—did today with Thomas Drake, another former N.S.A. employee, who, in 2010, was charged with espionage for revealing details about an electronic-eavesdropping project called Trailblazer, a precursor to Operation Prism, one of the programs that Snowden documented. (The felony cases against Drake, as my colleague Jane Mayer has written, eventually collapsed, and he pleaded guilty to a misdemeanor.)

INTERVIEWER: Not everybody thinks Edward Snowden did the right thing. I presume you do. . .

DRAKE: I consider Edward Snowden as a whistleblower. I know some have called him a hero, some have called him a traitor. I focus on what he disclosed. I don't focus on him as a person. He had a belief that what he was exposed to—U.S. actions in secret—were violating human rights and privacy on a very, very large scale, far beyond anything that had been admitted to date by the government. In the public interest, he made that available.

INTERVIEWER: What do you say to the argument, advanced by those with the opposite viewpoint to you, especially in the U.S. Congress and the White House, that Edward Snowden is a traitor who made a narcissistic decision that he personally had a right to decide what public information should be in the public domain?

DRAKE: That's a government meme, a government cover—that's a government story. The government is desperate to not deal with the actual exposures, the content of the disclosures. Because they do reveal a vast, systemic, institutionalized, industrial-scale Leviathan surveillance state that has clearly gone far beyond the original mandate to deal with terrorism—far beyond.

As far as I'm concerned, that about covers it. I wish Snowden had followed

Drake's example and remained on U.S. soil to fight the charges against him. But I can't condemn him for seeking refuge in a country that doesn't have an extradition treaty with the United States. If he'd stayed here, he would almost certainly be in custody, with every prospect of staying in a cell until 2043 or later. The Obama Administration doesn't want him to come home and contribute to the national-security-versus-liberty debate that the President says is necessary. It wants to lock him up for a long time.

And for what? For telling would-be jihadis that we are monitoring their Gmail and Facebook accounts? For informing the Chinese that we eavesdrop on many of their important institutions, including their prestigious research universities? For confirming that the Brits eavesdrop on virtually anybody they feel like? Come on. Are there many people out there who didn't already know these things?

Snowden took classified documents from his employer, which surely broke the law. But his real crime was confirming that the intelligence agencies, despite their strenuous public denials, have been accumulating vast amounts of personal data from the American public. The puzzle is why so many media commentators continue to toe the official line. About the best explanation I've seen came from Josh Marshall, the founder of T.P.M., who has been one of Snowden's critics. In a post that followed the first wave of stories, Marshall wrote, "At the end of the day, for all its faults, the U.S. military is the armed force of a political community I identify with and a government I support. I'm not a bystander to it. I'm implicated in what it does and I feel I have a responsibility and a right to a say, albeit just a minuscule one, in what it does."

I suspect that many Washington journalists, especially the types who go on Sunday talk shows, feel the way Marshall does, but perhaps don't have his level of self-awareness. It's not just a matter of defending the Obama Administration, although there's probably a bit of that. It's something deeper, which has to do with attitudes toward authority. Proud of their craft and good at what they do, successful journalists like to think of themselves as fiercely independent. But, at the same time, they are part of the media and political establishment that stands accused of ignoring, or failing to pick up on, an intelligence outrage that's been going on for years. It's not surprising that some of them share Marshall's view of Snowden as "some young guy I've never heard of before who espouses a political philosophy I don't agree with and is now seeking refuge abroad for breaking the law."

Mea culpa. Having spent almost eighteen years at *The New Yorker*, I'm arguably just as much a part of the media establishment as David Gregory and his guests. In this case, though, I'm with Snowden—not only for the reasons that Drake enumerated but also because of an old-fashioned and maybe naïve inkling that journalists are meant to stick up for the underdog and irritate the powerful. On its side, the Obama Administration has the courts, the intelligence services, Congress, the diplomatic service, much of the media, and most of the American public. Snowden's got Greenwald, a woman from Wikileaks, and a dodgy travel document from Ecuador. Which side are you on?

Edward Snowden Is No Hero

By Jeffrey Toobin
The New Yorker, June 10, 2013

Edward Snowden, a twenty-nine-year-old former C.I.A. employee and current government contractor, has leaked news of National Security Agency programs that collect vast amounts of information about the telephone calls made by millions of Americans, as well as e-mails and other files of foreign targets and their American connections. For this, some, including my colleague John Cassidy, are hailing him as a hero and a whistleblower. He is neither. He is, rather, a grandiose narcissist who deserves to be in prison.

Snowden provided information to the *Washington Post* and the *Guardian*, which also posted a video interview with him. In it, he describes himself as appalled by the government he served:

> The N.S.A. has built an infrastructure that allows it to intercept almost everything. With this capability, the vast majority of human communications are automatically ingested without targeting. If I wanted to see your e-mails or your wife's phone, all I have to do is use intercepts. I can get your e-mails, passwords, phone records, credit cards.

> I don't want to live in a society that does these sort of things. . . I do not want to live in a world where everything I do and say is recorded. That is not something I am willing to support or live under.

What, one wonders, did Snowden think the N.S.A. did? Any marginally attentive citizen, much less N.S.A. employee or contractor, knows that the entire mission of the agency is to intercept electronic communications. Perhaps he thought that the N.S.A. operated only outside the United States; in that case, he hadn't been paying very close attention. In any event, Snowden decided that he does not "want to live in a society" that intercepts private communications. His latter-day conversion is dubious.

And what of his decision to leak the documents? Doing so was, as he more or less acknowledges, a crime. Any government employee or contractor is warned repeatedly that the unauthorized disclosure of classified information is a crime. But Snowden, apparently, was answering to a higher calling. "When you see everything you realize that some of these things are abusive," he said. "The awareness of wrong-doing builds up. There was not one morning when I woke up. It was a natural process." These were legally authorized programs; in the case of Verizon Business's phone records, Snowden certainly knew this, because he leaked the very court order that approved the continuation of the project. So he wasn't blowing the whistle on anything illegal; he was exposing something that failed to meet his own standards of propriety. The question, of course, is whether the government can function when all of its employees (and contractors) can take it upon themselves to sabotage the programs they don't like. That's what Snowden has done.

What makes leak cases difficult is that some leaking—some interaction between reporters and sources who have access to classified information—is normal, even indispensable, in a society with a free press. It's not easy to draw the line between those kinds of healthy encounters and the wholesale, reckless dumping of classified information by the likes of Snowden or Bradley Manning. Indeed, Snowden was so irresponsible in what he gave the *Guardian* and the *Post* that even these institutions thought some of it should not be disseminated to the public. The *Post* decided to publish only four of the forty-one slides that Snowden provided. Its exercise of judgment suggests the absence of Snowden's.

Snowden fled to Hong Kong when he knew publication of his leaks was imminent. In his interview, he said he went there because "they have a spirited commitment to free speech and the right of political dissent." This may be true, in some limited way, but the overriding fact is that Hong Kong is part of China, which is, as Snowden knows, a stalwart adversary of the United States in intelligence matters. (Evan Osnos has more on that.)[1] Snowden is now at the mercy of the Chinese leaders who run Hong Kong. As a result, all of Snowden's secrets may wind up in the hands of the Chinese government—which has no commitment at all to free speech or the right to political dissent. And that makes Snowden a hero?

The American government, and its democracy, are flawed institutions. But our system offers legal options to disgruntled government employees and contractors. They can take advantage of federal whistleblower laws; they can bring their complaints to Congress; they can try to protest within the institutions where they work. But Snowden did none of this. Instead, in an act that speaks more to his ego than his conscience, he threw the secrets he knew up in the air—and trusted, somehow, that good would come of it. We all now have to hope that he's right.

Note

1.   http://www.newyorker.com/news/letter-from-china/can-edward-snowden-stay-in-hong-kong

The Snowden Principle

By John Cusack
The Huffington Post, June 14, 2013

At the heart of Edward Snowden's decision to expose the NSA's massive phone and Internet spying programs was a fundamental belief in the people's right-to-know. "My sole motive is to inform the public as to that which is done in their name and that which is done against them," he said in an interview with the *Guardian*.

From the State's point of view, he's committed a crime. From his point of view, and the view of many others, he has sacrificed for the greater good because he knows people have the right to know what the government is doing in their name. And legal, or not, he saw what the government was doing as a crime against the people and our rights.

For the sake of argument, this should be called The Snowden Principle.

When The Snowden Principle is invoked and revelations of this magnitude are revealed; it is always met with predictable establishment blowback from the red and blue elites of state power. Those in charge are prone to hysteria and engage in character assassination, as are many in the establishment press that have been co-opted by government access. When The Snowden Principle is evoked the fix is always in and instead of looking at the wrongdoing exposed, they parrot the government position no matter what the facts.

The Snowden Principle just cannot be tolerated. . .

Even mental illness is pondered as a possible reason that these pariahs would insist on the public's right to know at the highest personal costs to their lives and the destruction of their good names. The public's right to know—This is the treason. The utter corruption, the crime.

But as law professor Jonathan Turley reminds us, a lie told by everyone is not the truth. "The Republican and Democratic parties have achieved a bipartisan purpose in uniting against the public's need to know about massive surveillance programs and the need to redefine privacy in a more surveillance friendly image," he wrote recently.

We can watch as The Snowden Principle is predictably followed in the reaction from many of the fourth estate—who serve at the pleasure of the king.

Mika Brzezinski on MSNBC suggests that Glenn Greenwald's coverage was "misleading" and said he was too "close to the story." Snowden was no whistleblower, and Glenn was no journalist she suggests.

Jeffrey Toobin, at the *New Yorker*, calls Snowden "a grandiose narcissist who deserves to be in prison."

Another journalist, Willard Foxton, asserted that Glenn Greenwald amounted to the leader of a "creepy cult."

David Brooks of the *New York Times* accuses Snowden—not the Gov—of betraying everything from the Constitution to all American privacy. . .

Michael Grunwald of TIME seems to suggest that if you are against the NSA spying program you want to make America less safe.

Then there's Richard Cohen at the *Washington Post*, who as Gawker points out, almost seems to be arguing that a journalist's job is to keep government secrets, not actually report on them.

The Snowden Principle makes for some tortured logic.

The government's reaction has been even worse. Senators have called Snowden a "traitor," the authorities claim they're going to treat his case as espionage. Rep. Peter King outrageously called for the prosecution of Glenn Greenwald for exercising his basic First Amendment rights. Attacks like this are precisely the reason I joined the Freedom of the Press Foundation board (where Glenn Greenwald and Laura Poitras also serve as board members).

As Chris Hedges rightly pointed out, this cuts to the heart of one of the most important questions in a democracy: will we have an independent free press that reports on government crimes and serves the public's right to know?

It cannot be criminal to report a crime or an abuse of power. Freedom of the Press Foundation co-founder Daniel Ellsberg argues that Snowden's leaks could be a tipping point in America. This week he wrote "there has not been in American history a more important leak than Edward Snowden's release of NSA material," including his own leak of the Pentagon Papers.

The Snowden Principle, and that fire that inspired him to take unimaginable risks, is fundamentally about fostering an informed and engaged public. The Constitution embraces that idea. Mr. Snowden says his motivation was to expose crimes, spark a debate, and let the public know of secret policies he could not in good conscience ignore—whether you agree with his tactics or not, that debate has begun. Now, we are faced with a choice: we can embrace the debate or we can try to shut the debate down and maintain the status quo.

If these policies are just, then debate them in sunlight. If we believe the debate for transparency is worth having, we need to demand it. Snowden said it well, "You can't wait around for someone else to act."

Within hours of the NSA's leaks, a massive coalition of groups came together to plan an international campaign to oppose and fix the NSA spying regime. You can join them here (https://optin.stopwatching.us/) I already did. The groups span across the political spectrum, from Dick Armey's FreedomWorks to the Progressive Change Campaign Committee and longtime civil rights groups like ACLU, Electronic Frontier Foundation and Free Press.

As more people find out about these abuses, the outrage mounts and the debate expands. Many in the mainstream media have shown that the public can't count on them to stand up to internal pressure when The Snowden Principle is evoked to serve the national interest, and protect our core fundamental rights.

The questions The Snowden Principle raises when evoked will not go away. . . . How long do they expect rational people to accept using the word "terror" to justify and excuse ever expanding executive and state power ? Why are so many in our government and press and intellectual class so afraid of an informed public? Why are they so afraid of a Free Press and the people's right to know?

It's the government's obligation to keep us safe while protecting our constitution. To suggest it's one or the other is simply wrong.

Professor Turley issues us a dire warning:

> In his press conference, Obama repeated the siren call of all authoritarian figures throughout history: while these powers are great, our motives are benign. So there you have it. The government is promising to better protect you if you just surrender this last measure of privacy. Perhaps it is time. After all, it was Benjamin Franklin who warned that "those who would give up essential liberty to purchase a little temporary safety deserve neither liberty nor safety.

See what's happened already, in the short time only since the PRISM program was made public, here: https://freedom.press/blog/2013/06/leaks-are-vital-democracy-and-nsa-revelations-are-quintessential-example-why.

＊＊＊

John Cusack is an actor, filmmaker, and board member of journalism advocacy group Freedom of the Press Foundation.

Report Puts Snowden-Like Leaks as the No. 2 Threat to U.S. Security

By Ken Dilanian
The Los Angeles Times, January 29, 2014

WASHINGTON—Insiders like Edward Snowden who leak secrets about sensitive U.S. intelligence programs pose a potentially greater danger to national security than terrorists, America's spy chiefs warned Wednesday in their annual report to Congress on global security risks.

For the first time, the risk of unauthorized disclosures of classified material and state-sponsored theft of data was listed as the second-greatest potential threat to America in a review of global perils prepared by the U.S. intelligence community. The risk followed cyber attacks on crucial infrastructure but was listed ahead of international terrorism.

U.S. officials previously have said it will cost billions of dollars to repair or revamp communications surveillance systems in the wake of the disclosures by Snowden, a former contract employee at a National Security Agency listening post in Hawaii who began leaking classified documents to the media in June and who later fled to Russia.

Appearing before the Senate Intelligence Committee, James Clapper, the director of national intelligence, said the leaks represent the "most damaging theft of intelligence information in our history." He urged Snowden to return the material, saying he made "the nation less safe and its people less secure."

"We've lost critical foreign intelligence collection sources, including some shared with us by valued partners," Clapper said. "Terrorists and other adversaries of this country are going to school on U.S. intelligence sources, methods and tradecraft, and the insights that they are gaining are making our job much, much harder."

Army Lt. Gen. Michael Flynn, who directs the Defense Intelligence Agency, said the leaks had endangered the lives of intelligence operatives and troops. Matt Olsen, heads of the National Counterterrorism Center, said they had made it tougher to track Al Qaeda and its affiliates.

"What we've seen in the last six to eight months is an awareness by these groups. . . of our ability to monitor communications and specific instances where they've changed the ways in which they communicate to avoid being surveilled," Olsen said.

Investigators believe Snowden copied 1.7 million documents from NSA servers, the largest breach of classified material in U.S. history, although only a fraction have been disclosed so far. Last summer, a military judge sentenced Army Pvt. Chelsea Manning, who was born Bradley Manning, to 35 years in prison for sending 750,000 classified diplomatic cables, military field reports and other material to WikiLeaks.

Both Snowden and Manning have been condemned by critics as traitors and hailed by supporters as whistleblowers who exposed government wrongdoing.

Only critics spoke at the hearing. Senator Susan Collins (R-Maine), said the classified documents Snowden downloaded, if printed out, would form a stack more than three miles high.

"It is evident to me that most of the documents stolen by Mr. Snowden have nothing to do with the privacy rights and civil liberties of American citizens or even the NSA collection programs," she said. "They pertain to the entire intelligence community and include information about military intelligence, our defense capabilities, the defense industry."

Although President Obama has denounced Snowden's actions, he announced plans this month to increase judicial review of the NSA's collection of domestic telephone records and to limit eavesdropping on friendly foreign leaders, two of the programs Snowden exposed.

In an interview with German television this week, Snowden said he was seeking to thwart undemocratic mass surveillance by U.S. intelligence. He repeated his claim that an NSA analyst could tap anyone's email account, including that of the U.S. president, an assertion current and former NSA officials hotly deny.

The 27-page "Worldwide Threat Assessment of the U.S. Intelligence Community," a report required by Congress, does not mention Snowden by name. But it warns that others may seek to follow his example.

"Trusted insiders with the intent to do harm can exploit their access to compromise vast amounts of sensitive and classified information as part of a personal ideology or at the direction of a foreign government," it reads. "The unauthorized disclosure of this information to state adversaries, non-state activists or other entities will continue to pose a critical threat."

The report repeatedly cites Russia and China as the leading state intelligence threats, both for theft of digital data and for disruption of computer systems, and for more traditional espionage operations aimed at stealing secrets from the U.S. government, the defense industry and elsewhere.

"They seek data on advanced weapons systems and proprietary information from U.S. companies and research institutions that deal with energy, finance, the media, defense, and dual-use technology," the report says.

The report cites deepening concern about Al Qaeda splinter groups in Syria, Iraq, Yemen and parts of North Africa. But it says a major terrorist attack on America is increasingly unlikely.

The threat of complex, sophisticated and large-scale attacks from core Al Qaeda operatives against the U.S. "is significantly degraded," the report says, although it warns that the threat to U.S. facilities overseas has increased.

It says Iran has made "concessions on its nuclear program" in order to get relief from international sanctions in a six-month deal with six global powers. "We do not know if Iran will eventually decide to build nuclear weapons," the report says.

It adds that Iran has made technical advances that "strengthen our assessment that Iran has the scientific, technical and industrial capacity to eventually produce nuclear weapons. That makes the central issue its political will to do so."

Manning's Convictions and His Victory

By Amy Davidson
The New Yorker, July 20, 2013

In a hearing that opens on Wednesday, Colonel Denise Lind, a military judge, will decide whether to sentence Bradley Manning to a hundred and thirty-six years in prison or some lesser span of time. (There's no minimum.) As soon as the term is decided, she will subtract a hundred and twelve days—a sanction on the government for its illegal treatment of Manning during the months he was kept in solitary confinement. As big and as small as those numbers are, Manning, who gave hundreds of thousands of classified battlefield reports and diplomatic cables to WikiLeaks when he was a twenty-two-year-old Army specialist, won something on Tuesday, even as he was convicted of twenty counts ranging from theft of government property and computer fraud to half a dozen violations of the Espionage Act. Lind, who heard the case—Manning waived a trial by a military jury—acquitted him on the most serious charge, of aiding the enemy. That one carried a life sentence; it would also have set a dangerous precedent about what it means to harm the United States and to have a free press.

Lind also acquitted Manning of one Espionage Act charge related to a battlefield video from Afghanistan, and reduced the charges on another related to a video of troops in an Apache helicopter opening fire on the streets of Baghdad. Before his court martial, Manning told the government that he was willing to plead guilty to ten charges, whose sentences added up to twenty years in prison, without asking for a deal. The government turned him down in order to pursue its Espionage Act and aiding-the-enemy cases. It got a partial victory on the first, with an extra century of potential time for Manning—and however many degrees the climate for whistle-blowers chills as a result (two decades might have done the trick). That is more than unfortunate. But it was, at least, rebuffed when it came to aiding the enemy. The charge was always a stretch; the best precedent the government could come up with was a hundred and fifty years old, a case that arose in the context of the Union occupation of the Confederate-leaning city of Alexandria. As I wrote [elsewhere], the dubious legal logic behind the charge was that giving information to a non-enemy reporter that an undesirable person might eventually read, and be glad to see, amounted to being in league with the enemy—something that could apply to the work of any number of investigative reporters. (The prosecution acknowledged that its arguments applied as much to the *Times* as to WikiLeaks.)

There are necessary secrets; it is always the case, in a functioning democracy, that the government also tries to declare unnecessary ones, out of embarrassment or expediency, and that the press tries to keep it from doing so. The Obama Administration has been disrupting that balance with a series of leak investigations. The acquittal was a small push back.

The aiding-the-enemy charge had become an emotional, as well as a legal, crux of the case. It may have mattered most as a precedent, in terms of its effect on generations of sources and reporters—people trying to talk openly about wars a hundred and fifty years from now. But it was also about who Manning was, and what he was trying to do, when he decided that everybody ought to see the files he saw, and know what America was doing in its wars and in the world. So the acquittal was a victory in that way, too. "We won the battle, now we need to go win the war," Manning's lawyer, David Coombs, said, according to the *Washington Post*. "Today is a good day, but Bradley is by no means out of the fire." The immediate fire will be at the sentencing hearing.

One often hears that Edward Snowden, the N.S.A. leaker, is not really brave, because he is not back in the United States taking responsibility for his breach of government secrecy. That would be more convincing if the government had lied a little bit less about some of the programs he exposed—but put that train of thought aside. What did Manning get for his offer to take a serious measure of responsibility? (Twenty years in prison for something you did when you were twenty-two is not anything to dismiss.) Some consideration in the sentencing, one hopes. But what he got, until now, was to be the object of prosecutorial overreach, with a charge that involved speeches about his "evil" interest in harming his country—not just his criminality or his mistakes in telling its secrets, and not his hope, in one way or another, to make it slightly better.

A Message from Edward Snowden, One Year Later

American Civil Liberties Union, June 4, 2014

Below is an email ACLU supporters received from Edward Snowden this morning, one year to the day since *The Guardian* broke the first in a series of revelations exposing the breathtaking scope of U.S. government surveillance.

It's been one year.

Technology has been a liberating force in our lives. It allows us to create and share the experiences that make us human, effortlessly. But in secret, our very own government—one bound by the Constitution and its Bill of Rights—has reverse-engineered something beautiful into a tool of mass surveillance and oppression. The government right now can easily monitor whom you call, whom you associate with, what you read, what you buy, and where you go online and offline, and they do it to all of us, all the time.

Today, our most intimate private records are being indiscriminately seized in secret, without regard for whether we are actually suspected of wrongdoing. When these capabilities fall into the wrong hands, they can destroy the very freedoms that technology should be nurturing, not extinguishing. Surveillance, without regard to the rule of law or our basic human dignity, creates societies that fear free expression and dissent, the very values that make America strong.

In the long, dark shadow cast by the security state, a free society cannot thrive.

That's why one year ago I brought evidence of these irresponsible activities to the public—to spark the very discussion the U.S. government didn't want the American people to have. With every revelation, more and more light coursed through a National Security Agency that had grown too comfortable operating in the dark and without public consent. Soon incredible things began occurring that would have been unimaginable years ago. A federal judge in open court called an NSA mass surveillance program likely unconstitutional and "almost Orwellian." Congress and President Obama have called for an end to the dragnet collection of the intimate details of our lives. Today legislation to begin rolling back the surveillance state is moving in Congress after more than a decade of impasse.

I am humbled by our collective successes so far. When the *Guardian* and The *Washington Post* began reporting on the NSA's project to make privacy a thing of the past, I worried the risks I took to get the public the information it deserved would be met with collective indifference.

One year later, I realize that my fears were unwarranted.

Americans, like you, still believe the Constitution is the highest law of the land, which cannot be violated in secret in the name of a false security. Some say I'm a man without a country, but that's not true. America has always been an ideal, and though I'm far away, I've never felt as connected to it as I do now, watching the necessary debate unfold as I hoped it would. America, after all, is always at our fingertips; that is the power of the Internet.

But now it's time to keep the momentum for serious reform going so the conversation does not die prematurely.

Only then will we get the legislative reform that truly reins in the NSA and puts the government back in its constitutional place. Only then will we get the secure technologies we need to communicate without fear that silently in the background, our very own government is collecting, collating, and crunching the data that allows unelected bureaucrats to intrude into our most private spaces, analyzing our hopes and fears. Until then, every American who jealously guards their rights must do their best to engage in digital self-defense and proactively protect their electronic devices and communications. Every step we can take to secure ourselves from a government that no longer respects our privacy is a patriotic act.

We've come a long way, but there's more to be done.

—Edward J. Snowden, American

Sources of Discomfort: National Security Reporting in the Age of Leak Hunts

By Noreen Malone
The New Republic, June 20, 2013

It doesn't take a top-secret data-mining algorithm to tell you that national security reporting has changed in the years since 9/11. A would-be whistleblower is newly able to share vast amounts of classified information by simply tapping a mouse pad. The government, meanwhile, is more willing to deploy its own digital technology to hunt down and prosecute the leakers. One side effect of this reality, though, is decidedly low-tech: Within the small world of journalists who write about national security, there's a renewed embrace of what you might call artisanal information-gathering techniques. Or, as the spies they cover might call it, tradecraft.

A good lesson in poor tradecraft, as it happens, shows up in the government's affidavit for a search warrant against James Rosen, the Fox News reporter whose article containing a classified leak on North Korea prompted a criminal investigation. Investigators linked Rosen to his source because the pair swiped into and out of the State Department immodestly close to one another. Bad idea. "National security reporters are not nearly as clever as we think we are," says one such journalist. "As the leak investigations are showing, our tradecraft is really, really lame." (The Rosen case also inspired reporters to look a bit more closely at the government's security, revealing a useful work-around at the Pentagon: Badge swipes are not required at one particular turnstile in the building. Reporters have nicknamed it the Rosen entrance.[1])

It's not so surprising that the State Department would check the turnstile timestamps of its own headquarters. But the end of the post-Watergate, pre–Judith Miller détente between the media and the Justice Department has also changed perceptions about what reporters can safely do once they leave federal real estate. Bottom line: They need to step up their game. The average journalist's skill at avoiding scrutiny "is basically out of an episode of *Get Smart*," the reporter says. "And we at least have to raise it to the level of *The Wire*. Time to buy some burner phones."

Or not use phones at all. Even chatting about the weather over the phone with a source means possibly exposing them. Same goes for other electronic communications. The e-mails about National Security Agency waste and fraud that whistleblower Tom Drake sent a *Baltimore Sun* reporter were encrypted using Hushmail, which is supposed to ensure security. But he coughed up his passwords when he became the target of an investigation, giving the prosecutors access to an intact paper trail of messages that they used to charge him with violating the Espionage Act. (He ultimately pled to a lesser charge.)

Not that separating twenty-first-century reporters from their technology is going to be easy. One attendee at a recent University of California, Berkeley, conference on investigative journalism described national security reporting panelists as a bit confused about how it might even be *possible* to set up a face-to-face meeting without using the phone. A return to potted plants on balconies?

Savvy information-gathering in the face of executive branch leak-hunting, though, means changing even analog behavior. The legal department at one major newspaper instructs reporters to use Post-it notes—removable in the face of a subpoena—should they ever need to write a source's name in a notebook. One Pentagon reporter says he has taken to hiding the blue badge that identifies him as press when walking through the building, lest it scare off potential sources. (He has been stopped a couple times and asked to produce ID but now knows to swerve the other way when he sees a Segway-enabled security officer.)

Despite the difficulty, it's hard not to hear a small note of excitement when journalists start talking tradecraft. National security reporters tend to be people (mostly men) motivated by noble goals like bringing truth to the public—but they can also exhibit an almost boyish delight at the coolness of negotiating with, or acting like, spies.

In cracking down on reporters' sources, the Obama administration has also highlighted the value of another old-school discipline common to both journalism and espionage: understanding the psychology of the person passing you the information. Sure, most unauthorized leaks still come from the sorts of sources reporters have long known how to court—the ass-coverer, the bureaucratic infighter, the aggrieved also-ran. (Deep Throat was upset about being aced out at the FBI.) But cultivating the whistleblowers behind the big Bush/Obama-era scoops requires skills akin to running an asset-in-place in some distant dictatorship—you have to work them through understandable freak-outs about the riskiness of what they're doing.

"There's something inherently paranoia inducing about operating in a highly secret environment," says one national security magazine reporter. The reporter also offers a less charitable version: "They're almost always crackpots!" Leakers who reach out, unsolicited, are often convinced that their information is explosive. (It's usually not.) But even non-crackpots who become whistleblowers tend to be a little squirrelly by the time they reach out. They've tried all the proper internal channels and been denied. One reporter likens his job to that of a therapist. "Don't disagree with their point of view," advises another national security reporter. "I would not lie to them, but I wouldn't go out of my way to say, 'You're just wrong and stupid.' It's not unlike if you've got an uncle who always likes to discuss politics. You just say, 'I see your point.'"

In fact, whistleblowers like Edward Snowden—the source for this month's explosive stories about the National Security Agency's data-mining programs—are rarely radicals. Although leaking amounts to "an act of civil disobedience," according to one reporter, a colleague says leakers "tend to be fairly type-A people, who sometimes perceive that they have the weight of national security on their backs." All the same, facilitating that act can require some hand-holding.

In this culture of heightened scrutiny, journalists say their confidential sources are more eager than ever to see evidence of reporters' own bona fides. "Most of those people are pretty fucking paranoid," says a longtime reporter, who, like everyone else in this article, asked to remain anonymous. It's no accident: Reporters on these beats need skittish sources to trust them. Talking to another reporter on the record is a good way to jeopardize those relationships.

Sources' post–9/11 demands for spy-quality tradecraft can undercut reportorial glory in more substantive ways. One leaker gave a particularly explosive document to a reporter at the *Los Angeles Times* on the condition that the story not be published under the reporter's own name, thus ensuring that their relationship would outlast any investigation. (He lost the byline, got the story, and kept the source.) Another reporter says that he has had sources ask if he's willing to fight a subpoena for them—the national security reporting equivalent of "Say you love me!" and the kind of thing sources asked much less frequently before prosecutors put Judith Miller behind bars in 2005.

Sources, though, aren't the only ones looking for extra reassurance these days. One of the reporters I spoke to e-mailed me after our conversation. "An addendum: My colleagues listening in to our conversation said you were likely an FBI agent trying to ferret out our sources and methods." For the record, I'm not. But who knows who else might have been listening to our call?

Note

1. The day after this article hit newsstands, the Rosen entrance at the Pentagon was eliminated. The usually always-open turnstile at the River entrance was closed Tuesday morning, meaning there was no longer a way into the building without swiping. A Pentagon spokesman has not provided comment to The New Republic about whether the timing was related. *Update: The turnstile has since been reopened.*

Intelligence Security Initiatives Have Chilling Effect on Federal Whistleblowers, Critics Say

By Scott Higham
The Washington Post, July 23, 2014

In early April, Senator Charles E. Grassley summoned FBI officials to his Capitol Hill office. He said he wanted them to explain how a program designed to uncover internal security threats would at the same time protect whistleblowers who wanted to report wrongdoing within the bureau.

The meeting with two FBI officials, including the chief of the bureau's Insider Threat Program, ended almost as soon as it began. The officials said the FBI would protect whistleblowers by "registering" them. When Grassley's staff members asked them to elaborate, the FBI officials declined to answer any more questions and headed for the door.

"We're leaving," said J. Christopher McDonough, an FBI agent assigned to the bureau's congressional affairs office, said Senate staff members who attended the meeting.

The episode infuriated Grassley (Iowa), a leading advocate for whistleblowers in Congress and the ranking Republican on the Senate Judiciary Committee. Any effort to register whistleblowers, he said, would "clearly put a target on their backs."

The Insider Threat Program and a continuous monitoring initiative under consideration in the intelligence community were begun by the Obama administration after the leaks of classified information by former NSA contractor Edward Snowden and Army Pvt. Chelsea Manning, and the Navy Yard shootings by Aaron Alexis, who used his security clearance to gain access to the base.

The programs are designed to prevent leaks of classified information by monitoring government computers and employees' behavior.

Grassley said the episode with the FBI illustrates how federal agencies are setting up internal security programs without giving careful consideration to whether they could dissuade whistleblowers from coming forward.

"The Insider Threat Program has the potential for taking the legs out from underneath all of the whistleblower protections we have," Grassley said in a recent interview.

Greg Klein, the head of the FBI's Insider Threat Program, and McDonough, the congressional affairs agent, did not return calls seeking comment. An FBI spokesman said the bureau does not plan to register whistleblowers. He said there was a misunderstanding about the nature of the briefing with staff members for Grassley, Judiciary Committee Chairman Patrick J. Leahy (D-Vt.) and a law enforcement official who is assigned to the Senate panel. The spokesman noted that the FBI has a whistleblower training program for employees and a whistleblower protection office.

"We recognize the importance of protecting the rights of whistleblowers," FBI spokesman Paul Bresson said.

Grassley is part of a growing chorus of lawmakers on Capitol Hill and attorneys for whistleblowers who warn that the Insider Threat Program and the potential intelligence community initiative threaten to undermine federal workers' ability to report wrongdoing without retaliation.

Together, the programs cover millions of federal workers and contractors at every government agency.

In February, Director of National Intelligence James R. Clapper Jr. testified before the Senate Armed Services Committee that a system was being considered to continuously monitor the behavior of employees with security clearances "on the job as well as off the job."

A senior intelligence official said a continuous monitoring program, mandated under the Intelligence Authorization Act and signed into law by President Obama on July 7, is being set up and initially will include federal employees who hold top-secret security clearances. The official said there are no plans to monitor employees after hours while they are using non-government computer systems.

"I think it's time to put up the caution light here," said Senator Ron Wyden (D-Ore.), a member of the Senate Intelligence Committee.

While Wyden included a provision in the most recent Intelligence Authorization Act that would prohibit retaliation against whistleblowers, he said he remains concerned about the impact of the threat programs.

"This really has the potential for abuse, and I think it could have a chilling effect on the public's right to know and effective oversight of our government," Wyden said.

Dan Meyer, the head of the Intelligence Community Whistleblowing & Source Protection program, created last year as part of the Office of Intelligence Community Inspector General, said he is working to ensure that employees who want to report wrongdoing can do so anonymously and without reprisal.

"The critical thing is to maintain confidentiality," Meyer said. He said he is preparing training materials for intelligence officers and spreading the word that employees can come to him anonymously through third parties.

If an employee has verifiable information about wrongdoing, a presidential directive takes effect, providing employees with protection against retaliation.

"We are in the process of making a systematic, cultural change and getting everyone on board," Meyer said.

After Manning's disclosures to WikiLeaks four years ago, Obama signed Executive Order 13587, directing government agencies to assess how they handle classified information. On November 28, 2010, the Office of the National Counterintelligence Executive issued a memo to senior government agency officials, advising them to identify insider threats.

The memo suggested using psychiatrists and sociologists to assess changes in employees' behavior.

"What metrics do you use to measure 'trustworthiness' without alienating employees?" the counterintelligence office asked the agency chiefs. "Do you use a psychiatrist or sociologist to measure: relative happiness as a means to gauge trustworthiness? Despondence and grumpiness as a means to gauge waning trustworthiness?"

"It will only increase hostility between the government and really serious federal employees who are trying to improve the system," said Lynne Bernabei, a partner at Bernabei & Wachtel in Washington who has been representing whistleblowers for nearly 30 years. "Turning the security apparatus against its own people is not going to work."

Whistleblower lawyers said they understand the need to protect classified information but think some of the new programs go too far.

"There are legitimate reasons for employers to be on the lookout for people who might be leaking classified information, but this will obviously have a chilling effect on employees who might want to blow the whistle," said Jason Zuckerman, who served as the senior legal adviser to the U.S. Office of Special Counsel, the federal agency charged with protecting whistleblowers, and now represents whistleblowers nationwide.

Michael German, a former undercover FBI agent and whistleblower, called the Insider Threat Program a "dangerous" initiative.

"These agencies have long treated whistleblowers as security threats and this makes things even worse," said German, now a senior national security fellow at the Brennan Center for Justice at New York University School of Law.

Mark S. Zaid, a lawyer who specializes in representing whistleblowers in the intelligence community and the military, said the administration is moving too quickly.

"They are using a very big net to catch a few small fish, and they are going to hurt a lot of good people in the process," he said.

Supreme Court Weighs Whistleblower Protections

Justices Consider Balance of Whistleblower Rights Against National Security

By Jess Bravin
The Wall Street Journal, November 4, 2014

WASHINGTON—The Supreme Court on Tuesday considered how to balance federal whistleblower protections against national security in a case involving an air marshal who was fired for disclosing reduced protection on Las Vegas flights despite a potential terrorist threat.

The justices at oral arguments appeared largely sympathetic to the former air marshal, Robert MacLean, whose disclosure to a journalist forced the Transportation Security Administration to acknowledge a "mistake" and reverse course amid criticism from members of Congress. But some justices were concerned a broad reading of the Whistleblower Protection Act could leave officials powerless to punish disclosures in murkier situations where the information could endanger national security.

"The facts are very much in your favor here," Justice Sonia Sotomayor told Mr. MacLean's attorney, Neal Katyal. But she said a ruling that opened the door to less justifiable disclosures left her "troubled."

The case puts two legislative goals in conflict. To prevent terrorists and criminals from foiling security measures, the Aviation and Transportation Security Act allows officials to punish employees who disclose "sensitive security information" under some circumstances.

At the same time, the whistleblower law encourages federal employees to come forward with information that poses "a substantial and specific danger to public health or safety, if such disclosure is not specifically prohibited by law."

To reconcile the conflict, the case turns on whether the information Mr. MacLean disclosed was "specifically prohibited by law" from release, as the government contends, or, as Mr. MacLean argues, merely kept quiet under agency policies that don't qualify as "law."

The government's lawyer, Deputy Solicitor General Ian Gershengorn, argued the term "law" should be read broadly.

"Congress directed TSA to promulgate regulations prohibiting disclosures that would be detrimental to the security of transportation," Mr. Gershengorn said. He said that could include anything from "a flight crew's plans for dealing with a hijacking attempt to vulnerabilities in airport security systems to the kind of federal air marshal deployment information at issue in this case."

To rule against the government, Mr. Gershengorn warned, would effectively authorize any employee to "override TSA's expert judgment" based only on his or her own "reasonable belief about what public safety requires."

But Justice Antonin Scalia suggested that the solution should focus on protecting important information without providing too much discretion to "an agency that just doesn't want any whistleblower, doesn't want any criticism of what it's doing."

Mr. Katyal said the problem wasn't too many whistleblowers, but too few. "I think Congress each time has looked at this situation and has said every single time, we need more whistleblowers to come forward, because that's the human fail-safe against a machine bureaucracy," he said.

Yet it remains "really hard for someone like Mr. MacLean, other whistleblowers, to go to the media because they put their job at risk," Mr. Katyal said.

Mr. MacLean's case began in July 2003, when he and other air marshals were briefed on a potential terrorist plot to hijack U.S. airliners. The agency then sent the marshals a text message temporarily canceling assignments to Las Vegas flights for budgetary reasons.

Mr. MacLean protested to his superiors and the agency inspector general, to no effect. He then, as a confidential source, spoke to an MSNBC reporter who published a story.

The TSA later learned Mr. MacLean's identity after an employee recognized him, despite a disguise, when he appeared in a 2004 NBC Nightly News report complaining the agency's dress code made it too easy to spot air marshals aboard flights. He later was fired, and ever since has been trying to get his job back.

Bibliography

Benkler, Yochai. "The Dangerous Logic of the Bradley Manning Case." *The New Republic*, March 1, 2013; http://www.newrepublic.com/article/112554

Berman, Jillian. "Company Retaliation Against Whistleblowers Rises to All-Time High, Survey Finds." *Huffington Post*, January 6, 2012; http://www.huffingtonpost.com/2012/01/06/business-ethics-_n_1189110.html

Bernstein, Jake. "Inside the New York Fed: Secret Recordings and a Culture Clash." *Fortune*. September 26, 2014; http://fortune.com/author/jake-bernstein/

Bouville, Mathieu. "Whistle-blowing and Morality." *Journal of Business Ethics;* http://mathieu.bouville.name/education-ethics/Bouville-whistle-blowing.pdf

Browning, Lynnley. "The Perks of Being a Whistleblower." *Newsweek*, January 30, 2014.

Coll, Steve. "The Spy Who Said too Much." *The New Yorker*, April 1, 2013: http://www.newyorker.com/magazine/2013/04/01/the-spy-who-said-too-much

Dashiell, Eddith A. "Espionage and Sedition Acts of 1917–1918." *Immigration in America* Web site, October 18, 2011; http://immigrationinamerica.org/482-espionage-and-sedition-acts-of-1917-1918.html

Devine, Tom, and Tarek F. Maassarani. *The Corporate Whistleblower's Survival Guide* (San Francisco: Barrett-Koehler, 2011).

Drucker, Peter. "What Is 'Business Ethics'?" *National Affairs,* spring 1981; http://www.nationalaffairs.com/public_interest/detail/what-is-business-ethics

Editorial Board. "Edward Snowden, Whistle-Blower." *New York Times*, January 1, 2014; http://www.nytimes.com/2014/01/02/opinion/edward-snowden-whistle-blower.html?_r=0

Ehley, Brianna. "GAO Outs Justice for Not Protecting Whistleblowers." *Fiscal Times*, February 24, 2015; http://www.thefiscaltimes.com/2015/02/24/GAO-Outs-Justice-Not-Protecting-Whistleblowers

Ellsberg, Daniel. "Truths Worth Telling." *New York Times*, September 28, 2004; http://www.nytimes.com/2004/09/28/opinion/28ellsberg.html?_r=0

"Filing a Qui Tam Lawsuit." *Morgan & Morgan* Web site; https://www.whistleblowerattorneys.com/qui-tam-lawsuits

Foti, Catherine. "When Is a 'Whistleblower' Not Really a 'Whistleblower'?" *Forbes*. August 7, 2013; http://www.forbes.com/sites/insider/2013/08/07/when-is-a-whistleblower-not-really-a-whistleblower/

Galveston, W.W. "A Case for Clemency for Snowden." *The Economist*, January 10, 2014; http://www.economist.com/blogs/democracyinamerica/2014/01/whistleblowers-and-national-security.

Ganim, Sara. "Women Who Blew Whistle in Student-Athlete Cases and What Happened Next." *CNN*, January 9, 2014; http://www.cnn.com/2014/01/09/us/ncaa-athlete-literacy-whistle-blowers/index.html

Glazer, Myron Peretz, and Penina Migdal Glazer. *The Whistleblowers: Exposing Corruption in Government and Industry* (New York: Basic Books, 1989).

Goltein, Elizabeth. "A Mixed Message for National Security Whistleblowers." *Huffington Post*, December 22, 2012; http://www.huffingtonpost.com/elizabeth-goitein/obama-whistleblowers_b_1989629.html

Greenberg, Andy. *This Machine Kills Secrets: How WikiLeakers, Cypherpunks, and Hacktivists Aim to Free the World's Information* (New York: Dutton, 2012).

Harris, Savaria, and Mitka Baker. "Lessons from the Year of the Whistleblower: A Changing Regulatory Regime." *Inside Counsel*, January 16, 2015; http://www.insidecounsel.com/2015/01/16/lessons-from-the-year-of-the-whistleblower-a-chang

Hicks, Josh. "Sen. Charles Grassley Plans New Whistleblower-Protection Caucus." *Washington Post*, April 10, 2014; http://www.washingtonpost.com/blogs/federal-eye/wp/2014/04/10/sen-charles-grassley-plans-new-whistleblower-protection-caucus/

Higgins, Tim, and Nick Summers. "GM Recalls: How General Motors Silenced a Whistle-Blower." *Bloomberg Business*, June 18, 2014: http://www.bloomberg.com/bw/articles/2014-06-18/gm-recalls-whistle-blower-was-ignored-mary-barra-faces-congress

Holguin, Jamie. "Whistleblowers Honored by Time." *CBS News*, December 22, 2002; http://www.cbsnews.com/news/whistleblowers-honored-by-time/

Horton, Scott. "A Setback for Obama's War on Whistleblowers." *Harper's*, August 9, 2011; http://harpers.org/blog/2011/08/a-setback-in-obamas-war-on-whistleblowers/

Hunt, Linda. "The Challenges Women Whistleblowers Face." *International Business Research*, April 2010.

"In Praise of Whistleblowers." *The Economist*, January 10, 2002; http://www.economist.com/node/930052

"In Search of Honesty." *The Economist*, August 15, 2002; http://www.economist.com/node/1284261

Jansen, Bart. "Supreme Court Sides with Former TSA Air Marshal." *USA Today*, January 21, 2015; http://www.usatoday.com/story/news/2015/01/21/supreme-court-tsa-maclean-air-marshal-whistle-blower/22040645/

Johnson, Roberta Ann. *Whistleblowing: When It Works—And Why* (Boulder, CO: Lynne Rienner Publications, 2003).

Johnston, David Cay. "Hounding Whistleblowers Is Wrong." *Newsweek*, October 28, 2013; http://www.newsweek.com/hounding-whistleblowers-wrong-1164

Kleinhempel, Matthias. "Whistleblowers May Have Moral and Immoral Motivations." In Berlatsky, Noah, ed., *Whistleblowers* (Farmington Hills, MI: Greenhaven Press, 2012).

Kohn, Stephen Martin. "Rewards Give Whistleblowers a Motivation to Reveal Wrongdoing." In Berlatsky, Noah, ed., *Whistleblowers* (Farmington Hills, MI: Greenhaven Press, 2012).

Lee, Timothy B. "Daniel Ellsberg: 'I'm sure that President Obama would have sought a life sentence in my case.'" *The Washington Post*, June 5, 2013; http://www.washingtonpost.com/blogs/wonkblog/wp/2013/06/05/daniel-ellsberg-im-sure-that-president-obama-would-have-sought-a-life-sentence-in-my-case/

Madar, Chase. "Alleged WikiLeaks Whistleblower Bradley Manning Is a Hero." In Berlatsky, Noah, ed., *Whistleblowers* (Farmington Hills, MI: Greenhaven Press, 2012).

Madar, Chase. "The Trials of Bradley Manning." *The Nation*, July 31, 2013; http://www.thenation.com/article/175512/trials-bradley-manning.

Marks, Alexandra. "National Security vs. Whistleblowing." *Christian Science Monitor*, January 24, 2006; http://www.csmonitor.com/2006/0124/p02s01-uspo.html

Matthewson, Kirsty. "Ethics and Whistleblowing." Expolink Web site, January 10, 2012; http://expolink.co.uk/whistleblowing/blog/ethics-and-whistleblowing/

Mayer, Jane. "The Secret Sharer." *The New Yorker*, May 23, 2011; http://www.newyorker.com/magazine/2011/05/23/the-secret-sharer

McMillan, Michael. "Retaliation Against Whistle-Blowers: No Good Deed Goes Unpunished." *Enterprising Investor*, October 24, 2012; http://blogs.cfainstitute.org/investor/2012/10/24/whistle-blowing-no-good-deed-goes-unpunished/

Nadler, Judy, and Miriam Schulman. "Whistleblowing in the Public Sector." Markkula Center for Applied Ethics, Santa Clara University Web site; http://www.scu.edu/ethics/practicing/focusareas/government_ethics/introduction/whistleblowing.html

O'Donnell, Jayne. "Whistle-blowers Form a Breed Apart." *USA Today*, July 29, 2004; http://usatoday30.usatoday.com/money/companies/management/2004-07-29-whistle-blower-main_x.htm

O'Neill, Ben. "The Ethics of Whistleblowing." Mises Institute Web site, July 8, 2013; http://mises.org/library/ethics-whistleblowing

Penny, Brian. "Why You Should Encourage Whistleblowing at Your Company." *Fast Company*, May 30, 2014; http://www.fastcompany.com/3031223/5-ways-to-actually-make-whistleblowing-work-for-your-business

Press, Eyal. "Whistleblower, Leaker, Traitor, Spy." *New York Review of Books*, August 5, 2013; http://www.nybooks.com/blogs/nyrblog/2013/aug/05/whistleblower-leaker-traitor-spy/

Radack, Jesselyn. "Whistleblowers Expose Illegal Activity, Not Government Secrets." In Berlatsky, Noah, ed., *Whistleblowers* (Farmington Hills, MI: Greenhaven Press, 2012).

Ravishankar, Lilanthi. "Encouraging Internal Whistleblowing in Organizations." Markkula Center for Applied Ethics, Santa Clara University Web site; http://www.scu.edu/ethics/publications/submitted/whistleblowing.html

Reid, Brad. "Whistleblower Statutory Protections Are Frequently Narrowly

Interpreted by Courts." *Huffington Post*, November 13, 2014; http://www.huffingtonpost.com/brad-reid/whistleblower-statutory-p_b_6154148.html

Sagar, Rahul. *Secrets and Leaks: The Dilemma of State Secrecy* (Princeton, NJ: Princeton University Press, 2013).

Savage, Charlie. "Official Backs Marines' Move to Classify Photos of Forces with Taliban Bodies." *New York Times*, June 10, 2014; http://www.nytimes.com/2014/06/11/us/official-backs-marines-move-to-classify-photos-of-forces-with-taliban-bodies.html?_r=0

Schoenfeld, Gabriel. "Those Who Expose National Secrets Should be Punished." In Berlatsky, Noah, ed., *Whistleblowers* (Farmington Hills, MI: Greenhaven Press, 2012).

Schwellenbach, Nick. "Why Military Whistleblowers Fear Reprisal." *Time*, October 20, 2011; http://nation.time.com/2011/10/20/why-military-whistleblowers-fear-reprisal/

Shafer, Jack. "Live and Let Leak." *Foreign Affairs*, March/April 2014.

Shorrock, Tim. "Obama's Crackdown on Whistleblowers." *The Nation*, March 26, 2013; http://www.thenation.com/article/173521/obamas-crackdown-whistleblowers?page=0,0

Smith, Andrew. "'There Were Hundreds of Us Crying out for Help': The Afterlife of the Whistleblower." *The Guardian*, November 22, 2014; http://www.theguardian.com/society/2014/nov/22/there-were-hundreds-of-us-crying-out-for-help-afterlife-of-whistleblower

Solomon, Norman, and Marcy Wheeler. "The Government War Against Reporter James Risen." *The Nation*, October 8, 2014; http://www.thenation.com/article/181919/government-war-against-reporter-james-risen?page=0,3

Taibbi, Matt. "A Whistleblower's Horror Story. *Rolling Stone*, February 18, 2015; http://www.rollingstone.com/politics/news/a-whistleblowers-horror-story-20150218?page=2

Tate, Julie. "Bradley Manning Sentenced to 35 Years in WikiLeaks Case." *Washington Post*, August 21, 2013; http://www.washingtonpost.com/world/national-security/judge-to-sentence-bradley-manning-today/2013/08/20/85bee184-09d0-11e3-b87c-476db8ac34cd_story.html

Tugend, Alina. "Opting to Blow the Whistle or Choosing to Walk Away." *New York Times*, September 20, 2013.

Van Buren, Peter. "Edward Snowden's Long Flight Home." *The Huffington Post*, July 1, 2013; http://www.huffingtonpost.com/peter-van-buren/edward-snowden-flight_b_3528401.html

Vukovic, Adam. "Corporate Whistleblower Protection and the Sarbanes-Oxley Act." *LegalMatch*, December 12, 2014; http://www.legalmatch.com/law-library/article/corporate-whistleblower-protection-and-the-sarbanes-oxley-act.html

Waytz, Adam, James Dungan, and Liane Young. "The Whistle-Blower's Quandary." *New York Times*, August 2, 2013; http://www.nytimes.com/2013/08/04/opinion/sunday/the-whistle-blowers-quandary.html

Whistleblowing-CEE Web site. "What Is Whistleblowing?" (http://www.whistle-blowing-cee.org/about_whistleblowing/)

Wilentz, Sean. "Would You Feel Differently about Snowden, Greenwald, and As-sange if You Knew What They Really Thought?" *The New Republic*, January 19, 2014;   http://www.newrepublic.com/article/116253/edward-snowden-glenn-greenwald-julian-assange-what-they-believe

Websites

Amnesty International

amnesty.org.uk

Amnesty International is an organization broadly devoted to "standing up for humanity and human rights." They work to educate and mobilize the public and to expose and fight against abuses. They have worked to support and defend whistleblowers who have come under attack for publicizing abuses of power and injustices in both the private and public sector.

Electronic Frontier Foundation

https://www.eff.org/

The Electronic Frontier Foundation is a leading nonprofit organization devoted to defending civil liberties in the digital world. "Founded in 1990, EFF champions user privacy, free expression, and innovation through impact litigation, policy analysis, grassroots activism, and technology development." They also lead the fight against the National Security Agency's mass surveillance program

Freedom of the Press Foundation

https://freedom.press/

Co-founded by famous whistleblower and publisher of the Pentagon Papers Daniel Ellsberg, Freedom of the Press Foundation is devoted to the support and defense of "public-interest journalism focused on exposing mismanagement, corruption, and law-breaking in government." In addition to developing encryption tools for journalists, it also accepts and provides donations to individual whistleblowers and other whistleblower advocacy organizations who are devoted to transparent journalism and in need of support.

Government Accountability Project (GAP)

whistleblower.org

The Government Accountability Project is a leading supporter of whistleblowers, and is devoted to their advocacy and protection. "A non-partisan public-interest group, GAP litigates whistleblower cases, helps expose wrongdoing to the public, and actively promotes government and corporate accountability. Since its founding in 1977, GAP has helped over 6,000 whistleblowers."

National Whistleblowers Center

http://www.whistleblowers.org/

The National Whistleblowers Center (NWC) is an organization that works to advance the rights of whistleblowers by providing support and legal assistance. "Since 1988, the NWC, whistleblowers supported by the NWC and attorneys representing these whistleblowers have achieved victories for environmental protection, government contract fraud, nuclear safety and government and corporate accountability."

Occupational Safety & Health Administration's Whistleblower Protection Program

http://www.whistleblowers.gov/

OSHA's Whistleblower Protection Program enforces the whistleblower provisions of more than twenty whistleblower statutes protecting employees who report violations of various workplace safety and health laws. Since passage of the OSH Act (Occupational Safety and Health Act) in 1970, Congress has expanded OSHA's whistleblower authority to protect workers from discrimination under twenty-two federal laws. Complaints must be reported to OSHA within set timeframes following the discriminatory action, as prescribed by each law.

U.S. Securities and Exchange Commission (SEC) Office of the Whistleblower

https://www.sec.gov/whistleblower

The Office of the Whistleblower was established to administer the SEC's whistleblower program. Whistleblowers who know of possible securities law violations can provide assistance and information to the Commission and, through their knowledge of the circumstances and individuals involved, help identify possible fraud and other violations much earlier than might otherwise have been possible. Through this office, the Commission strives "to minimize the harm to investors, better preserve the integrity of the United States' capital markets, and more swiftly hold accountable those responsible for unlawful conduct."

Whistleblowing Network

whistleblowingnetwork.org

Whistleblowing Network (WIN) "connects and strengthens civil society organizations that defend and support whistleblowers. The Network provides counsel, tools and expertise needed by those working in their countries to address corruption, waste, fraud, abuse, illegality and threats to the public interest."

Wikileaks
wikileaks.org

The website that whistleblower Julian Assange made famous, WikiLeaks is a not-for-profit media organization whose goal is to publicize important news and information. Through their secure website (or electronic drop box), sources can anonymously leak information to this organization's journalists who then publish original source material alongside their news stories "so readers and historians alike can see evidence of the truth." Since its official launch in 2007, WikiLeaks has also developed and adapted technologies that support the safe leaking and publishing of information, and in the face of legal and political attacks, have continued this work, based in the "broader principles" including the "[defense] of freedom and media publishing, the improvement of our common historical record and the support of the rights of all people to create new history."

Index